Improving Teacher Education

Eva C. Galambos, *Editor*
Consultant, Southern Regional Education Board

NEW DIRECTIONS FOR TEACHING AND LEARNING
KENNETH E. EBLE, *Editor-in-Chief*
University of Utah, Salt Lake City

Number 27, Fall 1986

Paperback sourcebooks in
The Jossey-Bass Higher Education Series

Jossey-Bass Inc., Publishers
San Francisco • London

LB
1715
.I43x

Eva C. Galambos (Ed.).
Improving Teacher Education.
New Directions for Teaching and Learning, no. 27.
San Francisco: Jossey-Bass, 1986.

New Directions for Teaching and Learning
Kenneth E. Eble, *Editor-in-Chief*

Copyright © 1986 by Jossey-Bass Inc., Publishers
and
Jossey-Bass Limited

Copyright under International, Pan American, and Universal Copyright Conventions. All rights reserved. No part of this issue may be reproduced in any form—except for brief quotation (not to exceed 500 words) in a review or professional work—without permission in writing from the publishers.

New Directions for Teaching and Learning is published quarterly by Jossey-Bass Inc., Publishers.

Editorial correspondence should be sent to the Editor-in-Chief, Kenneth E. Eble, Department of English, University of Utah, Salt Lake City, Utah 84112.

Library of Congress Catalog Card Number 85-81906

International Standard Serial Number ISSN 0271-0633

International Standard Book Number ISBN 1-55542-994-7

Cover art by WILLI BAUM

Manufactured in the United States of America

Ordering Information

The paperback sourcebooks listed below are published quarterly and can be ordered either by subscription or single-copy.

Subscriptions cost $40.00 per year for institutions, agencies, and libraries. Individuals can subscribe at the special rate of $30.00 per year *if payment is by personal check.* (Note that the full rate of $40.00 applies if payment is by institutional check, even if the subscription is designated for an individual.) Standing orders are accepted.

Single copies are available at $9.95 when payment accompanies order, and *all single-copy orders under $25.00 must include payment.* (California, New Jersey, New York, and Washington, D.C., residents please include appropriate sales tax.) For billed orders, cost per copy is $9.95 plus postage and handling. (Prices subject to change without notice.)

Bulk orders (ten or more copies) of any individual sourcebook are available at the following discounted prices: 10-49 copies, $8.95 each; 50-100 copies, $7.96 each; over 100 copies, *inquire.* Sales tax and postage and handling charges apply as for single copy orders.

Please note that these prices are for the academic year 1986-1987 and are subject to change without prior notice. Also, some titles may be out of print and therefore not available for sale.

To ensure correct and prompt delivery, all orders must give either the *name of an individual* or an *official purchase order number.* Please submit your order as follows:

Subscriptions: specify series and year subscription is to begin.
Single Copies: specify sourcebook code (such as, TL1) and first two words of title.

Mail orders for United States and Possessions, Latin America, Canada, Japan, Australia, and New Zealand to:
> Jossey-Bass Inc., Publishers
> 433 California Street
> San Francisco, California 94104

Mail orders for all other parts of the world to:
> Jossey-Bass Limited
> 28 Banner Street
> London EC1Y 8QE

New Directions for Teaching and Learning Series
Kenneth E. Eble, *Editor-in-Chief*

TL1 *Improving Teaching Styles,* Kenneth E. Eble
TL2 *Learning, Cognition, and College Teaching,* Wilbert J. McKeachie
TL3 *Fostering Critical Thinking,* Robert E. Young
TL4 *Learning About Teaching,* John F. Noonan

TL5 *The Administrator's Role in Effective Teaching,* Alan E. Guskin
TL6 *Liberal Learning and Careers,* Charles S. Green III, Richard G. Salem
TL7 *New Perspectives on Teaching and Learning,* Warren Bryan Martin
TL8 *Interdisciplinary Teaching,* Alvin M. White
TL9 *Expanding Learning Through New Communications Technologies,* Christopher K. Knapper
TL10 *Motivating Professors to Teach Effectively,* James L. Bess
TL11 *Practices that Improve Teaching Evaluation,* Grace French-Lazovik
TL12 *Teaching Writing in All Disciplines,* C. Williams Griffin
TL13 *Teaching Values and Ethics in College,* Michael J. Collins
TL14 *Learning in Groups,* Clark Bouton, Russell Y. Garth
TL15 *Revitalizing Teaching Through Faculty Development,* Paul A. Lacey
TL16 *Teaching Minority Students,* James H. Cones III, John F. Noonan, Denise Janha
TL17 *The First Year of College Teaching,* L. Dee Fink
TL18 *Increasing the Teaching Role of Academic Libraries,* Thomas G. Kirk
TL19 *Teaching and Aging,* Chandra M. N. Mehrotra
TL20 *Rejuvenating Introductory Courses,* Karen I. Spear
TL21 *Teaching as Though Students Mattered,* Joseph Katz
TL22 *Strengthening the Teaching Assistant Faculty,* John D. W. Andrews
TL23 *Using Research to Improve Teaching,* Janet C. Donald, Arthur M. Sullivan
TL24 *College-School Collaboration: Appraising the Major Approaches,* William T. Daly
TL25 *Fostering Academic Excellence Through Honors Programs,* Paul G. Friedman, Reva Jenkins-Friedman
TL26 *Communicating in College Classrooms,* Jean M. Civikly

Contents

Editor's Notes 1
Eva C. Galambos

Chapter 1. The Current Status of General Education for Teachers 5
Eva C. Galambos

A survey of transcripts of over three thousand graduates of major universities in Southern states reveals the extent of general education in students' preparation for public school teaching.

Chapter 2. Extending Teacher Preparation Programs 17
Dale P. Scannell

During the past fifty years, significant changes have occurred in the expectations of schools and in our knowledge of the teaching/learning process. The four-year model for teacher education is no longer adequate for the comprehensive teacher education programs now necessary.

Chapter 3. The Risks and Inadequacy of Extended Programs 27
Willis D. Hawley

Extending teacher preparation programs to five years entails too great a cost, denies resources to other educational reforms, and does not necessarily improve either teacher competence or the status of the profession.

Chapter 4. Public School and Teacher Education Reform: A Proposal for Shared Action 37
Phillip C. Schlechty, Betty Lou Whitford

Public schools must play a more central role in teacher education than they do now. What is needed is an organization separate from public schools, the university, and the teachers' organizations that can act as an effective force for teacher professionalization.

Chapter 5. A Bold "Old" Step: Return to Laboratory Schools 49
Ernest K. Dishner, Paula R. Boothby

Laboratory schools offer an ideal setting for innovation and systematic educational inquiry. Despite the decline in the number of laboratory schools after World War II, these schools serve needs that are still strongly present in American public school education.

Chapter 6. Integrating the Clinical Approach into Pedagogy Courses 59
Norma Nutter

Educational theory and practical experience are central to teacher education, since neither is adequate in itself. Teacher education must combine theory and practice, admonition and example, ideas and realistic experience in an integrated, carefully planned curriculum.

Chapter 7. The Reduction in Teacher-Preparation Institutions: 69
Rationale and Routes
Hendrik D. Gideonse
Instructional resources for teacher preparation are too thinly distributed and improperly structured to justify the numbers of institutions now engaging in such programs. The next decades should see a real and substantial reduction in the number of teacher preparation programs and institutions.

Chapter 8. Private Liberal Arts Colleges and Teacher Preparation 83
Norene F. Daly
The traditional orientation of liberal arts colleges toward teaching continues to make them major contributors to teacher education. The commitment these colleges make to teacher education and the governance structure that helps them devise and carry out effective programs argue strongly for supporting teacher education in the liberal arts colleges.

Chapter 9. Common Directions Toward Improvement 91
Eva C. Galambos
Amidst much criticism of public school education, what consensus can be found on how to improve the preparation of teachers?

Index 101

Editor's Notes

This volume on how to improve the preparation of teachers comes at a time of great turmoil in teacher education. As documented by several authors, the last two years have been marked by an avalanche of recommendations by commissions and task forces at national, regional, and state levels. These recommendations pull teacher education in various directions.

After years of debate, the national accreditation standards for teacher education programs were revised in 1985. However, a number of states have changed their teacher certification rules and now allow applicants who have not completed teacher education programs into the teaching profession. This anomaly between a profession that seeks to tighten its preparation standards and the public's action to bypass the profession's regular entry route is another signal that this is an opportune moment to examine teacher preparation. Concerns that reappear in the various contributions of this volume revolve around (1) how to strengthen subject area preparation, (2) what is the necessary length of time for preservice preparation of teachers, (3) how to address theory and research as well as how to include the practice of teaching in learning how to teach, and (4) what existing or new institutions will educate teachers most effectively.

Chapter One (by the editor) deals with "content" or subject area preparation, including general education for all teachers and academic majors and minors for secondary teachers. The looseness of the general education requirements in many institutions has eroded the foundation in liberal arts for many students. If there is truth in the accusation that education courses represent watered-down material with little intellectual challenge, perhaps this is all that can be expected when students complete a weak lower division program.

In Chapter Two, Scannell justifies the need for extended programs (five or more years) for entry into teaching. Longer time is needed to accommodate content preparation, professional studies, as well as the practice of teaching skills. In institutions where extended programs have been established, more attention can be given to the pedagogical knowledge base that is emerging from new research on effective teaching. Since the longer time to prepare teachers reflects the imperatives of the material to be covered, Scannell proposes that extended programs become the predominant model of the future.

In response, Hawley in Chapter Three opposes the move to five-year programs for two major reasons: (1) higher costs, which will further exacerbate the quantity-quality problems of teacher supply, and (2) lack of evidence that extended programs will produce more effective teachers. Hawley points to the necessity for research to provide evidence on the effectiveness of various teacher education models before any wholesale decisions are made or major costs are incurred. He suggests a deregulated environment in which various models of teacher education might be tried and then evaluated. Such evaluation would also apply to the new alternative programs that provide pedagogical assistance only after the employment of teachers with degrees in arts and sciences.

Schlechty and Whitford, in Chapter Four, recognize that teachers learn to teach by teaching, not by sitting in college classrooms. The role of higher education in preparing teachers is to ensure that teachers master the content to be taught as well as the education-related subjects, such as child development and research on effective schools. Higher education, however, is not very good at teaching people how to perform on the job. Schlechty and Whitford suggest shifting most of a teacher's professional preparation to a new setting that is outside of the exclusive control of either higher education or the schools. A new "academy" is needed, wherein master teachers and faculty from universities could collaborate in preparing teachers as they actually teach. Such an academy would probably be established within an existing school system.

Dishner and Boothby, and Nutter take different approaches in Chapters Five and Six as they, too, consider ways to increase the opportunities for future teachers to apply theory to practice. Dishner and Boothby suggest a return to laboratory schools for pre-student teaching experience. They do not, however, propose to shift the student teaching courses to lab schools. The availability of lab schools for early and frequent observation of children, mini-teaching, and other types of field experience would increase the opportunities for practical applications of theory. They also suggest that educational research would be more fruitful if undertaken as collaborative efforts by faculty in a long-range plan and that lab schools facilitate such work. They connect proposals to establish a national academy on teaching to a regional network of lab schools.

Nutter, too, stresses practical applications of theory in the pedagogical portion of teacher education. She suggests numerous techniques that education faculty should employ to ensure that students are practicing what they read about or hear in lectures. The existing configuration of teacher education programs offers many opportunities for creative integration of the "clinical" approach in pedagogy courses to bridge theory and practice, although this strategy, too, will entail some added costs.

Gideonse and Daly in Chapters Seven and Eight tackle the question of which institutions are best suited to produce effective teachers. Gideonse calls for a serious reduction (possibly by as much as two-thirds) from the some 1,250 colleges and universities that now prepare teachers. He compares the new standards for teacher education programs with the resources available to programs and concludes that the vast majority cannot possibly meet these standards. The only way to ensure quality, he concludes, is to eliminate many programs.

Many of the programs with limited resources are in the private and independent liberal arts colleges, which do contribute to the supply of new teachers. Daly points out the advantages such institutions offer for preparing teachers. It is in these colleges that one finds communication and collaboration between education and arts and sciences faculties. In the large state universities, the two groups of faculty seldom interact. The liberal arts colleges cannot afford to offer a wide array of electives, but this seeming disadvantage results in a more cohesive general education curriculum for all students, including teachers. Current suggestions for reform that require even elementary teachers to complete an academic major are already implemented at and inherent in the nature of these colleges.

Finally, in Chapter Nine the editor seeks to discern common threads in the various contributions that point the way toward a consensus on needed directions for improving teacher education.

Eva C. Galambos
Editor

Eva C. Galambos is consultant to the Southern Regional Education Board. She served as staff director of that organization's Task Force on Higher Education and the Schools from 1981 to 1985.

A more rigorous general education sequence of courses in the liberal arts at the college level is necessary to strengthen teacher preparation—that is, within the confines of the baccalaureate.

The Current Status of General Education for Teachers

Eva C. Galambos

This chapter deals primarily with the general education of teachers as determined from the transcripts of 3,283 1982-1983 graduates of major universities in Southern states. The largest producer of teachers in each of the fourteen states was included plus three other universities that wished to participate (Galambos and others, 1985). The "flagship" university of six states was included in the study. Each of these graduates completed an approved teacher education program.

In focusing on the general rather than the pedagogical aspect of teacher education, this chapter differs from recent critiques of teacher education. For example, although the widely disseminated report of the National Commission for Excellence in Teacher Education (1985, p. 11) does call for "the integration of liberal studies" in its description of a total preparation program, its treatment of general education is cursory. The Commission mentions specifically that general education should include courses in sociology, anthropology, psychology and knowledge and understanding of literature, history, language, and the arts; but strangely enough, it fails to mention mathematics or science.

Why the Emphasis on General Education?

A sound foundation in liberal studies is especially important for future teachers. Primary grade teachers function as generalists, who can enrich the curriculum—if they are liberally educated. Take, for instance, a vocabulary lesson. A generalist might allude not only to specific meaning and spelling, but also to origin, related words, and usage in various times and settings. An example may illustrate the excitement a liberally educated teacher can bring even to a spelling lesson. Take the word "impediment," defined as an obstruction or hindrance. The word could open many vistas. Caesar describes his conquest of Gaul (Who was Caesar? Where is Gaul?) and wrote of *impedimenta*. In Latin this means "baggage." Clearly, that was a hindrance in crossing the Alps (Where are they?). The root of the word clarifies other words: *im* implies the negative. *Ped* means foot, which leads to the word pedestrian. One could go on. The point is, how could a youngster forget such a lesson or be bored?

Although the curriculum in the secondary schools is segmented by subjects, there, too, teachers are recognizing the need to integrate subject matter across courses. Writing across the curriculum is an outstanding example. In the past five years the message is increasingly penetrating that all teachers must practice writing—the first step in helping their students to improve writing skills. How many teachers today wish they had spent more time (probably in general education) on composition or at least on evaluating the quality of writing in their readings!

Another rationale for more emphasis on general education for all college students (regardless of their majors) is that it provides a foundation for upper level courses. The quality (depth and breadth) of upper level courses depends on whether students can read with comprehension at the college level—that is, can evaluate and compare what they read and can use deductive and inductive reasoning. Only if students develop these skills in lower division courses will they perform at or participate in collegiate studies that may truly be classified as upper level work.

There is now agreement that education majors should be exposed to the emerging research on effective teaching. What is the likelihood of their ability to evaluate research studies? At the minimum, they must understand statistical significance. To do so, a college-level statistics course is necessary—one that covers more than means and mediums.

On a more pragmatic note: A sound foundation in the liberal arts (or general education) is necessary for passage of teacher certification tests. Inability to perform on the general education portions, rather than on the professional education or specialty area, of the National Teacher Examination is the more frequent problem for those who fail to pass the test (Louisiana Board of Regents, 1981).

The high correlation (R=.88) between SAT scores of 3,344 North

Carolina baccalaureates and their common-core National Teacher Examination scores four years later is evidence of the importance for teachers of verbal and mathematical skills (Ayres, 1982). These are the subjects in which students receive instruction in postsecondary studies during the sophomore and freshman curriculum. Since communication and quantitative skills are weaker for education majors than for arts and sciences majors (Weaver, 1979), rigorous general education coursework that covers these areas is even more critical.

While teacher educators stress that knowledge of subject is no insurance that a teacher will be effective in the classroom, it has become almost trite to point out that teachers cannot teach what they do not know. One cognitive characteristic of teachers has been shown to be related to students' learning outcomes. In the study that still represents the most comprehensive analysis of student outcomes, Coleman (1966) found that most achievement differences were accounted for by socio-economic factors. But the verbal ability of teachers as measured by vocabulary tests was an important variable in explaining differential learning once socio-economic variables were standardized. It is difficult to conceive that general education could be unrelated to vocabulary skills.

How to Define General Education

The percentage that general education comprises of the total baccalaureate program for teachers ranges from 30 to 40 percent, depending on the source. Ishler (1984) surveyed 103 institutions that are members of the Association of Colleges and Schools of Education in State Universities and Land Grant Colleges and Affiliated Private Universities to determine requirements for graduation. For the 66 responding institutions, general education averages 51 and 47 semester hours for elementary and secondary education majors, respectively. The range for elementary education programs is 33 to 81 hours, and for secondary, 30 to 65 hours.

The National Commission for Excellence in Teacher Education reports that approximately 40 percent of the program "is made up of general liberal arts coursework, similar to that taken by students in other majors" (National Commission for Excellence in Teacher Education, 1985, p. 13). The median requirement for those states with clearly stated standards who responded to a National Education Association survey of state certification standards falls within the range of 33 to 37 percent of total baccalaureate credits (Feistritzer, 1983).

Some of the numerical variation regarding general education semester hours requirements reflects differences in the definitions of general education. The definition adopted for the Southern Regional Education Board transcript study is a function both of logic and of the shape of the data that were used in the study.

The following assumption was used: Any arts and sciences course that a student took as part of the baccalaureate degree (in transfer credits or at the degree-granting university), except courses in the student's major, constitutes general education. In other words, English courses taken by a chemistry major constitute general education for the chemistry major but not for the English major. By the same logic, chemistry courses taken by the English major constitute general education for the English major but not the chemistry major. For an elementary education major, all arts and sciences courses constitute general education.

Transcripts shed no light on whether a student takes a course as an elective or as a requirement for the general core. It is impossible from a transcript to differentiate whether Literature 202 represents completion of a humanities requirement or an elective. From the standpoint of general education, it makes no difference. Either reason for taking any arts and sciences course can result in general education.

How Much General Education

To evaluate the amount and kind of general education, earned semester credits shown on each transcript were coded course by course. This was done for the graduates eligible for teacher certification, and also to provide a point of reference, for a sample of 2,760 arts and sciences graduates. Each of the 17 participating universities supplied a randomly drawn sample of its arts and sciences graduates in 1982–1983, stratified by disciplines. (The results of coding these credits are summarized in Table 1.)

In four of the five major divisions of general education, teachers completed fewer credits than liberal arts graduates. In mathematics, science, English, and other liberal arts, teachers completed the equivalent of three three-semester credit courses less than the arts and sciences graduates. The largest differences were in "other liberal arts," accounted for largely by foreign languages, which future teachers avoid. (Three-fourths

Table 1. Average General Education Hours (Percent of Total Credit)

	Teachers Credit Hours	Teachers Percent of Total Credits	Arts and Sciences Credit Hours	Arts and Sciences Percent of Total Credits
Mathematics	6.0	4.2	7.2	5.2
Science	11.6	8.2	12.2	9.1
English	11.3	8.0	11.8	8.8
Social science	21.6	15.3	20.4	15.0
Other liberal arts	11.4	8.1	17.8	13.4

of teachers take no foreign languages at all, as compared to one-third of arts and sciences graduates.)

Offset against the lesser number of credits in four divisions of general education were the slightly more hours taken by teachers in social sciences. This greater number results directly from courses in psychology. (Some institutions offer educational psychology in the psychology department, which results in the course being coded as arts and sciences.) In all other social sciences, teachers complete fewer credits than arts and sciences graduates—in history, political sciences, economics, sociology, and other social sciences combined (which include anthropology and geography).

The average number of hours taken by teachers in economics is 0.9. Political science, presumably the discipline that includes American government, fares only slightly better with an average of 2.2 semester hours. In the sciences, teachers gravitate toward biology. They shun physics and chemistry. Almost two-thirds of the teachers took no chemistry or physics, compared with one-half of arts and sciences graduates.

English and mathematics are two disciplines in which colleges offer remedial courses for poorly prepared students. Credits for courses labeled remedial were coded only when transcripts showed credits had been awarded. A small percentage of both teachers and arts-and-sciences graduates earned such credits—for remedial English, 4 percent of teachers and 2 percent of other graduates; for mathematics, 3 percent of both groups.

The more surprising finding is that 7 and 11 percent of teachers, and arts and sciences groups respectively, took no mathematics at all—either in community colleges, in the senior institutions, or as advanced placement credit needed to exempt them from college math courses.

What Level of Coursework

Since mathematics is the one discipline in which course entrance prerequisites are usually quite clearly specified in the catalogue, it is a discipline that lends itself to analyzing the level of coursework. When prerequisites specify that the student must have completed Algebra I and II and Geometry prior to entry, the course is clearly a college-level offering. Mathematics courses other than remedial and clearly college-level courses were coded in two other categories. These are identified below, with examples of the catalogue descriptions for such courses.

1. Mathematics for Elementary Teachers:
   201 *Understanding Arithmetic* (3 semester hours). Open only to students seeking elementary certification. Concepts stressed over manipulation. Set and functions, whole numbers, integers, numeration, elementary number theory.

202 *Understanding Elementary Mathematics* (3 semester hours). Prerequisite: 201. Continuation of MAT 201: rational numbers, decimals and real numbers, geometry, measurement, metric system.

2. Noncollege Level Mathematics (not requiring prior completion of Algebra I, II, and Geometry):
Basic Concepts of Mathematics (3 semester hours). Designed primarily for liberal arts students who do not intend to take advanced courses in mathematics. Mathematics is approached from a cultural-historical point of view, with emphasis on ideas and their significance rather than on manipulative processes or computations. Topics from number theory, algebra, geometry, topology, and analysis are included.

Only 16 percent of the teachers (versus 55 percent of the arts-and-sciences graduates) took at least one college-level mathematics course. For teachers, only 22 percent of their total math credits represent college-level math, as compared to 53 percent of arts-and-sciences graduates.

The argument that teachers must address not only the content of mathematics but also how it is to be taught in classrooms is valid and explains why courses are offered in education colleges on methods of presenting content. Indeed, elementary education majors in the SREB study completed, on the average, nineteen semester hours in courses offered by colleges of education on the techniques and materials of teaching specific subjects, including methods of teaching mathematics. Since the "how to" is covered in the "methods" courses, why should content courses also be offered in sections that are limited to teachers? Should mathematics for teachers end with whole numbers, fractions, and decimals, while other college students learn about probabilities, functions, and matrix algebra?

Mathematics courses comprise only 4 to 5 percent of total credits teachers and arts-and-sciences graduates earn during their baccalaureate program. Thus, so much scrutiny of such a small portion of the program may seem unwarranted. Yet, it is the one discipline that lends itself to a qualitative analysis of the expected level of work for college students from a perusal of catalogue course descriptions. The fact that such a small proportion of teachers (and only half of the arts and sciences graduates) complete college-level courses in mathematics leads to the question of whether their work in other disciplines is more rigorous.

There are some indications of problems in other divisions of general education. In English, the average number of credits earned that specify "composition" is 3.2 semester hours. Two-thirds of teachers transferred credits from community or other colleges. English is, of course, one of the subjects most frequently taken in community college. If it were known whether the transferred English courses included substantial composition components, perhaps the total time future teachers devote to practicing writing might have been seen to exceed the average of 3.2 credit hours. One would hope so.

The average number of English credits that graduates complete is more than the normal general education requirement. So perhaps the almost four three-semester-hour or three four-hour courses completed include English electives, perhaps in literature. But such electives are certainly not upper-level courses. Less than one hour of upper-level English coursework, on the average, is included in teachers' transcripts. Philosophy is very unpopular; less than one hour average is taken of lower- or upper-level courses. To the extent that ethics and values are important issues for future teachers, why is so little philosophy taken when its study could indicate how mankind has dealt with these problems in the past?

Teachers take more fine arts courses—applied fine arts—than arts-and-sciences graduates. Art and music history and appreciation courses show up less frequently on teachers' transcripts. Economics is shunned; three-fourths of teachers and 60 percent of arts-and-sciences graduates avoid it altogether. Sociology, anthropology, and psychology are of interest to more teachers. These disciplines are more akin to the issues with which teachers will deal, such as the breakdown of the family, cultural differences, and child development. Yet these topics are also covered in education courses, of which teachers take many hours. The "foundations" courses, for example, are often described as dealing with social and cultural aspects of education.

Elementary teachers will spend the majority of their time with children in the early grades on language arts and arithmetic. Yet as college students, these teachers complete less time in academic courses in these two disciplines combined than in social science.

The Distribution Requirements

The statistical results as well as the general impression of coding over 6,000 transcripts indicate that many students gravitate to courses that deal with familiar subjects and shun what is new to them. This is hardly a liberating experience. The looseness of the general education distribution requirements in some institutions allows students to avoid areas of the curriculum. Of the seventeen major universities in the transcript study, six may be characterized as prescriptive and are fairly specific about listing the courses students may take to meet the distribution requirements in each of the five major academic divisions. The list of permitted courses to fulfill the division requirements is not very long.

At the other extreme are eight free choice institutions that are not specific about course requirements. Students have wide latitude in choosing a given minimum number of hours across four or five major divisions. If courses are listed that meet the division requirements, the choice may be so wide as to include all courses in a discipline from 100 to 299. Another characteristic of the free choice group is that mathematics, foreign languages, philosophy, or various combinations of these disciplines may be taken interchangeably to meet a divisional requirement. An example of a requirement that exemplifies free choice is the natural science requirement that reads: "Biology, chemistry, computer science, mathematics, physical science, physics—three one-semester courses; each course must be from a different discipline." This applies in a total baccalaureate program with a minimum of 120 semester hours.

Between these two extremes are three institutions that do circumscribe student choice to some extent but not as much as the prescriptive institutions. For example, one institution does specify the courses that may be taken to meet each of the divisional requirements, but the list is extremely long. The nine quarter-hours in social sciences, in addition to the traditional introductory courses in all the major social science disciplines, also include environmental problems, family relationships, and criminology. Since these three courses are offered by three different departments, they would conceivably seem to meet the social science requirement.

The institutions vary tremendously in their general education mathematics requirements for the bachelor of arts. In only seven of the seventeen institutions is mathematics explicitly required as part of general education for all degrees or majors. In some institutions mathematics is mentioned only as an option, along with other disciplines, to meet a divisional requirement. Thus, for a bachelor of arts degree, courses in mathematics, languages, computer sciences, and even history of science may be taken to satisfy the division requirement. (For the bachelor of science degree, however, mathematics is usually specified as a separate divisional requirement.) Three institutions offer a choice between a philosophy or mathematics course; logic may be the specified philosophy course, but this is not always the case.

In the absence of a pervasive requirement in mathematics, it is not surprising that in the transcript study the average number of hours and level of mathematics taken by graduates were so low, and that a substantial proportion of the graduates took no mathematics at all. The requirements in the majority of institutions are loose enough to permit these outcomes.

There is more prescriptiveness among the seventeen institutions on completion of science courses than there is on mathematics. Fourteen specify that some science courses must be taken, and half of these indicate that one or more courses must include a laboratory. Three institutions group science with other disciplines for the purpose of academic division requirements, giving students a choice as to whether they take any science at all.

Only five institutions specify that the division requirement must include both biological and physical sciences or at least two different disciplines. Two institutions take the opposite tack: They require that the minimum hours be completed as a sequence in one science. The remaining ten institutions allow leeway about how students spread those requirements across one or more science disciplines.

In social science, of the seventeen institutions only three require that U.S. history be included as part of the social science divisional requirement. These same three institutions also specify in their catalogues that a course shall be taken in U.S. government. One additional institution specifies that the divisional requirement in history must include a course in Western history. Five of the seventeen institutions require foreign language for students pursuing the bachelor of arts.

How to Get More General Education into a Baccalaureate

Anyone who bemoans the shortcomings of the preparation of teachers is obligated to suggest constructive alternatives. Given the pressures of time, is it reasonable to expect more "content" courses in a baccalaureate program, while still including sufficient instruction in the theory of pedagogy and practice of teaching skills? Or is the answer to extend the total education beyond the traditional four years?

There has been a tendency in the United States to prolong formal education. This trend is evident across many fields, ranging, for example, from physicians to medical technicians, or from MBA's to legal secretaries (as paralegals with associate degrees). (Engineers, remarkably, have resisted the trend.) From a labor market perspective, keeping entrants out of the market for longer periods while they complete more years of education may have made sense when the baby boom generation inflated the supply of professionals. Today, when college graduates are declining in absolute numbers and when the older, near-retirement group is a growing segment of the work force, the need for workers may well reverse the trend for longer college preparation. The projected shortage of teachers is a signal of this labor market phenomenon. Indeed, the teaching profession may have missed its opportunity to extend the length of preparation by seeking to implement the policy at a time of shortage rather than surplus.

As to whether longer preparation is needed to provide competent teachers, one must consider the entire sequence of preservice education. If high school graduates complete a weak program with too little emphasis on rigorous courses, as emphasized by the 1980 reformers, then college becomes a catch-up time for high school work. The transcript study indicates that such has been the case for many students. Students are taking college courses that cover content that should have been mastered in high school. If this mode of college work continues, then extending formal education may be necessary. If the freshman year is a catch-up year, then five years of college may be needed to cover what is expected in a normal baccalaureate program.

An honest approach to this situation—and one that will restore the prestige of the college degree—is to provide remedial work in college but not label it as college work. A five-year sequence may be needed, but the award should not masquerade as a degree of higher level than the baccalaureate.

If the courses students take in college are truly college level, is there enough time to cover content and pedagogy in teacher preparation? The results of the transcript study lend credence to this possibility. The configuration of the average total credits earned by the elementary teachers in the transcript study is shown in Table 2.

If all of the sixty-nine semester hours now spent in general education (plus some of the nineteen hours devoted to methods courses) were spent in college-level work in English, mathematics, social science, science, and other liberal arts, then elementary teachers could obtain a solid liberal education and have at least forty-nine remaining semester hours to devote to pedagogy courses and physical education. This would still vastly exceed the thirty semester hours in education courses that comprise the average requirement in the certification regulations of the Southern states.

By freeing up the baccalaureate from some of the forty-nine education credits (which vastly exceed credits in most arts and science majors) and by drawing on those courses in general education that are introductory for arts and sciences majors, elementary teachers might even pursue a major within the baccalaureate. Certainly, in the alternative, there is enough time within the course it now takes elementary teachers to earn a bachelor's degree for them to gain more exposure to various academic subjects—provided that general education means college-level work.

Table 2. Elementary Teacher Education Programs

		Current Average Credit Hours
General Education		69.3
Education Courses		49.4
Methods	18.8	
Field Application	16.4	
Other Courses	14.2	
Physical Education and Transferred Education and/or Physical Education		9.0
Other Courses		9.2
Total Credits		136.9

The general conclusion of the transcript study is that the current four-year education of teachers should be tightened and made more rigorous. Only when this has been accomplished and after a cadre of teachers has become available who have completed rigorous baccalaureates from which the remedial and the "fluff" have been eliminated, will the consideration of an extended preparation program be timely.

References

Ayres, Q. W. "Racial Desegregation, Higher Education, and Student Achievement." *Journal of Politics*, May 1982, pp. 337-365.

Coleman, J. *Equality of Educational Opportunity*. Washington, D.C.: Office of Education, U.S. Department of Health, Education, and Welfare, 1966.

Feistritzer, E. C. *The Condition of Teaching*. Princeton, N.J.: The Carnegie Foundation for the Advancement of Teaching, 1983.

Galambos, E. C., Cornett, L. M., and Spitler, H. D. *An Analysis of Transcripts of Teachers and Arts and Sciences Graduates*. Atlanta: Southern Regional Education Board, 1985.

Ishler, R. E. "Requirements for Admission to and Graduation from Teacher Education." *Phi Delta Kappan*, October 1984, pp. 121-122.

Louisiana Board of Regents. *The Regents Report*, October 7, 1981.

National Commission for Excellence in Teacher Education. *A Call for Change in Teacher Education*. Washington, D.C.: American Association of Colleges for Teacher Education, 1985.

Weaver, T. "In Search of Quality: The Need for Talent in Teaching." *Phi Delta Kappan*, September 1979, pp. 29-46.

Eva C. Galambos is consultant to the Southern Regional Education Board. She served as staff director of that organization's Task Force on Higher Education and the Schools from 1981 to 1985.

More comprehensive teacher education programs are required to provide adequate attention to the liberal arts and teaching field content and to enhance what is known about effective teaching.

Extending Teacher Preparation Programs

Dale P. Scannell

The prevailing model for teacher education in this country has remained relatively constant for over fifty years. The typical four-year baccalaureate program provides that two years be devoted primarily to general education and two years be split between coursework in the field to be taught and professional education—pedagogy. This model has prevailed for more years than has any other in the evolution of teacher education and longer than the models found in virtually all other fields of professional preparation.

During the past fifty years, significant changes have occurred in our society, in our expectations of schools and in our knowledge about factors that affect the teaching/learning process. Fifty years ago most children completed schooling in the community where they started elementary school. The mores of a given community were relatively monolithic and were understood and accepted by citizens of that community. Most children grew up in homes with two resident parents, one of whom was at home to greet the child at the end of the school day. Teachers were among those who were best educated in the community and were respected, even if patronized in some ways. Education's role was relatively narrow, with an emphasis on academic subjects.

In contrast, great mobility now characterizes our society; it is unusual for a child to attend school in the same district from kindergarten through the twelfth grade. Most communities have populations that represent a variety of life-styles and value systems. The church, the community, and even the family provide less nurturance and structure for youth. Many children live with single parents or with parents in their second or third marriages. Schools have become instruments for implementing public policy and for social change. In response, school curricula have been expanded to include health, career, economic and parent education, and among many other topics, drug and alcohol abuse education. All of these changes affect the role of teachers and the preparation required for teachers to meet their responsibilities. However, teachers are still educated, to a large extent, in a model that may have been sufficient fifty years ago but certainly is not today. Teacher education has not evolved in step with the rest of society.

Recent Criticism of Teacher Education

During the past several years, a large number of national, state, and regional commissions and task forces have issued reports on the condition of education. All decry deficiencies or ineffectivenesses of schools and teachers. Several criticize teacher education as a major factor related to teacher inadequacy and what is considered poor student achievement. Most of this group of critics call for reform of teacher education and a few recommend alternative certification for people who have not been educated to become teachers.

Arguments can be developed and evidence presented to refute some aspects of the criticism. Schools and teachers have responded to equity concerns, and they have provided educational opportunities for a larger number and percentage of school-age youth than ever before. Even though these criticisms may be exaggerated or misdirected, the current level of antagonism and dissatisfaction should cause teacher educators and policymakers to look seriously at teacher education and draw both empirical evidence and rational analyses to evaluate teacher education programs.

There are students of teacher education who respond to this criticism by pointing out, quite correctly, that the brightest and best educated teachers will experience difficulty in schools with high pupil-teacher ratios, poor facilities and instructional resources, bad discipline, and low expectations of achievement. Some note, further, that poor salary and working conditions drive the best teachers from teaching to more rewarding fields with better opportunities for advancement. Their conclusion places emphasis on improving the conditions for teachers in the work place rather than on improving teacher education. Why a choice between the two must be made has never been satisfactorily explained.

There are others who support efforts for reforming teacher education within the format of the four-year baccalaureate model and oppose lengthening programs until such efforts have been tested (Gallegos, 1981; Galambos, 1985). They point to the need for higher admission standards and more rigorous retention and graduation standards. Certification testing and internships for beginning teachers frequently are also advocated. The opponents of extended programs who urge the directions noted above include, among others, people from four-year and high-tuition institutions. Although reform of four-year curricula and more rigorous standards undoubtedly would improve the existing model, the question remains whether these reforms would be adequate, particularly in terms of the potential teachers have for guiding student development, both academic and personal. In addition, it should be noted that curriculum reform and more rigorous standards are characteristic of the extended programs already adopted; the more comprehensive programs require more talented students and the goal is to provide a more rigorous program to students who have the talent to profit from it.

Throughout higher education for the past few years, institutions have been engaged in intensive introspection stimulated primarily from grave concerns about the erosion of the liberal arts in baccalaureate degree programs. Several national reports on this theme appeared during the 1984–1985 academic year, recommending that the liberal arts (general studies) be strengthened in all programs even if some professional programs would then have to be extended to five years (NIE, 1984; AAC, 1985; NASULGC, 1984). The fields mentioned specifically include architecture, business, engineering, and *education.*

Following the enactment of Public Law 94-142, a large number of institutions did a comprehensive review of teacher education programs to identify the absence of those topics that are important to teachers in least restrictive environment classrooms (Sharp, 1982). An intrinsic part of the curriculum review was an attempt to eliminate redundancy among courses and to create space for the addition of new topics. Even when unnecessary duplication was eliminated, institutions had difficulty in accommodating mainstreaming materials in their programs. The common results were the addition of a course or a compromise on what was added to the curriculum. In addition to this one very important new requirement for teacher education, other issues require attention, such as multicultural education, classroom management, and the use of technology. On a rational basis, it seems unlikely that reform of four-year programs will be sufficient to achieve the full potential of teacher education.

The Common Features of Extended Programs

Four institutions have made comprehensive changes by extending all teacher education programs to five years. A large number of institutions have extended individual programs, such as special education, but do not adopt the extended format for all programs. The first comprehensive change was made at Austin College in Sherman, Texas, in 1971. The second was the University of New Hampshire in 1975. These were followed by changes at the University of Kansas in 1981 and the University of Florida in 1984. Austin is a small liberal arts institution; the other three are state supported. The latter two are large, complex institutions with a school and a college of education, offering most fields of study at all degree levels.

The four extended programs differ in several ways, including the organization of course work and the distribution of hours across the domains that comprise teacher education. However, the programs have much in common. In all four institutions, the decision was motivated by the belief that four years was insufficient to include adequate attention to the liberal arts, teaching field content, practical experience to translate theories into teacher behavior, and professional study to reflect what is known about the teaching/learning process. In all four institutions, these aspects are more adequately covered in the five-year program than in the four-year program they replaced.

In these programs the first two years of study focus almost entirely on the liberal arts distribution required for baccalaureate degrees. It should be noted that this requirement for prospective teachers approximates or exceeds that for students majoring in a liberal arts discipline.

Teaching field requirements in these institutions have undergone the least expansion in the extended program, primarily because strong teaching field requirements existed prior to the change. The requirements are similar to those for arts and science majors in terms of the amount of work required. Some differences exist to ensure that prospective teachers take courses that will enhance instruction in grades K–12.

Early experience for students in school settings is another common feature of the programs. Although differences exist in the amount and nature of field experiences, the extended programs recognize the importance of early career decisions and the orientation of prospective teachers to the teacher's role. All four programs also recognize the critical nature of simulation, peer teaching, and assignments in schools, which provide articulation between theory and practice. All four reflect the belief that students need "hands-on" experience prior to the student teaching or practicum assignment.

The programs are designed to reflect the knowledge base of teacher education more completely than was possible in the more restricted four-year programs. Many writers of the past few years—Gage (1978, 1984), B. O. Smith (1980), D. C. Smith (1983), and Berliner (1984), among others—have discussed the research findings on effective schools and classrooms and the pedagogical skills that influence the efficacy of the teaching/learning process. All four extended programs include a more thorough introduction for prospective teachers to the research literature and the skills that have been demonstrated to be important.

The existence of at least four different approaches to extended programs is undoubtedly fortuitous in the evolution of teacher education. These four approaches represent different attempts to accomplish similar goals and they provide a setting for comparative evaluations—information that will prove useful to other institutions in planning an approach to more comprehensive teacher education.

How Pervasive Will Extended Programs Become?

Traditionally there have been differences among elementary, secondary, and special education and K-12 teacher education programs. One might ask whether extended programs are needed in all of these various programs. Although there are different reasons across these programs, in all cases a rationale exists for extended programs.

Programs for elementary teachers have been criticized for overemphasis on methods at the expense of depth in an academic field. Recently there have been recommendations that elementary teacher education programs include at least two solid academic minors (AACTE, 1976, 1983; Gideonse, 1982). This reflects the recognition that elementary teachers are responsible for many subjects, and a common school practice is to assign teachers responsibility in one or two subjects for several classes and grades. However, some writers have suggested that all prospective teachers should have depth in at least one field to the extent that they understand how new knowledge in the field is created (AACTE, 1983).

Elementary teachers work with several subject areas and with a widely varying talent pool and also frequently interact with parents and school specialists. Thus, elementary teachers need breadth and depth in academic fields and in the pedagogical skills required for these subjects. In addition, they must have a wide repertoire of skills for working with pupils ranging from gifted to learning disabled. For their work with parents and specialists they need interpersonal skills and a working knowledge of specialty areas. To include education for these responsibilities within a program based solidly on a liberal arts foundation requires more time than four years.

Secondary education programs typically include solid majors in an academic field and programs thin in pedagogy. Whether extended programs are needed for prospective secondary teachers depends in part on the role assigned to secondary schools. If one is willing to view secondary education as college preparatory or as a series of alternative programs with a predominant homogeneous grouping, then a weaker base exists for extended secondary education programs. However, if secondary education is to prepare people for life as well as further education, that is, personally as well as academically or in a comprehensive high school setting, then extended programs are important.

Two points are central to this matter. First, if secondary teachers are expected to help all students reach their potential, then skills for individualizing planning, instruction, and evaluation are necessary. Second, in many high schools, a teacher must teach in at least two fields. To encompass at least a solid minor and a complete major, the liberal arts base, and pedagogy required for effective teachers, a program of more than four years is needed.

It is probably easiest to develop a rationale for extended programs for special education. In many states graduate work is required for full certification in special education, in recognition of the unique challenges that face these teachers. Special education programs must include many features of elementary programs—breadth in academic areas, a good liberal arts base, work in interpersonal relationships, and pedagogical skills. In addition, the special education literature is extensive and covers the areas of diagnosis, prescription, individualizing instruction, behavior management, and the use of technology in instruction. To include all these essential components, a program of more than four years is needed.

Art, music, and physical education are commonly offered in programs leading to K-12 certification. Thus, such programs include many features of both elementary and secondary programs. Art and music, in many institutions, are not really covered in four years and require more than 130 semester hours of work in approved programs. In such cases, the certification program is already semi-extended. The rationale for an extended-time secondary program applies to K-12 programs.

Strong arguments can be made for the importance of all of the typical initial certificate program areas. However, these arguments presume that teachers are seen as change agents, with responsibility for personal and academic development and for guiding all children and youth to realize their potential.

Extended Programs: A Limited or Predominant Model?

One of the arguments against extended programs in teacher education has frequently been that, while it may be appropriate (or at least acceptable) for some institutions to adopt extended models, it should not be required for all. This observation is based on the premise that four-year models are adequate as they currently exist.

The current move toward five-year programs is not an attempt to develop an *ideal* approach. Rather, it is an attempt to provide experiences that are *necessary* for effective and safe classroom performance and to establish a basis for continuing professional development of teachers. Some teacher education advocates, such as B. O. Smith (1980) and Cremin (1977), have recommended that teacher education be extended to six years.

The adoption of five-year models has involved serious risks for those institutions that have taken this step. Being motivated by the belief that the four-year program is inadequate, these institutions are constrained by the pragmatic restrictions of what their institutions would support and what potential students would accept.

The approval and acceptance of teacher education programs should always include standards important to the welfare of the students. Decisions about program content and length should not be based on institutional survival or convenience.

The question of what constitutes an adequate teacher education program also has serious political overtones. Teacher education programs are found in approximately 1,300 institutions, many of which are colleges and universities that have evolved from normal schools and teacher colleges. Many are four-year institutions. Many institutions have seriously limited resources; many are large, with commitments to the sciences, humanities, or prestigious professions. For these institutions a move to extend teacher education programs would be inconvenient and would require a change in institutional priorities. For four-year colleges, acceptance of extended programs would alter the role they currently play in the education of prospective teachers.

Does the evidence justify the adoption of more rigorous standards for teacher education that might require more comprehensive programs and thus entail more than four years of study? For those who favor an affirmative answer to this question, the scenario of the future includes the adoption of extended programs as the predominant model.

For institutions that offer postbaccalaureate programs and for those with adequate resources, extended teacher education programs will require some decisions regarding reallocation of priorities and resources. However, a movement toward extended programs should not jeopardize these institutions. For the four-year institutions, a restructuring of the role of teacher education might be required. Four-year institutions have an illustrious record in preparing students for advanced degree study and for postbaccalaureate professional schools. A number of colleges have developed articulation agreements with institutions that offer baccalaureate professional programs in business, architecture, engineering, and pharmacy. These take the form of 3-2, 4-1, or even 2-3 arrangements, in which the liberal arts part of the program is taken at the college. It is not unusual for these programs to include degrees from both institutions, a B.A. from the college and a B.S. from the institution offering the professional work.

Models similar to those in other fields could be developed in teacher education. The college could offer the liberal arts, and in some cases the teaching area content and the early professional foundations work. Consortium arrangements or articulation agreements could provide a smooth transition for students. If extended programs become widespread, the changes noted here undoubtedly will occur. Liberal arts colleges have a history of attracting talented students who want a small school environment or unique approach to a college. A move toward a different role in teacher preparation will not jeopardize a good liberal arts college.

The Teacher Shortage

In the late 1950s and early 1960s, education literature included frequent articles related to the need for extended teacher education programs. The expanding K-12 enrollments at that time, and the consequent need for large numbers of new teachers, undoubtedly was a significant reason why the extended program "movement" did not receive serious or sustained support.

During the 1970s when teacher supply was more than adequate to meet the demand, there always seemed to be some reason why the time was not propitious for considering extended programs. Now we are again facing a potential shortage of teachers. Is it socially irresponsible to consider extended programs at a time when schools need help in staffing classrooms?

The economic condition of the profession relates to this question. If more highly qualified individuals enter the teaching ranks, it would seem reasonable that higher salaries would be justified. In part, higher salaries may be necessary to attract talented individuals into extended teacher education programs. How can schools already facing economic pressures offer higher salaries to all teachers?

Aspects of the current school reform movement might offer an answer to these questions. The concepts of differentiated staffing and differential salary schedules (merit salary) each have appealing features, but in addition to improving the reward system for teachers, they could also contribute to more effective schools. The master teacher concept has a direct application to the way in which extended programs can feasibly contribute to school improvement within an economic system.

Research literature supports the importance of student-adult interaction as a factor in the learning and achievement process. As a result many schools now use teacher aides and paraprofessionals to relieve teachers of subprofessional duties and to participate under supervision in the instructional process. This practice can be increased, as it undoubtedly would be if all teachers were more competent in the professional aspects of school operations. The salaries for professional teachers could be increased in proportion to the increase in the ratio of pupils to professional teacher. At the same time, more paraprofessionals would be included in a professional team that would work under supervision and within a narrowly defined set of responsibilities for which they were trained.

If paraprofessionals and aides were used more extensively, a move to extended programs would not exacerbate the teacher supply-demand problem. In fact, extended programs would supply the type of teachers required in the current reform movement.

Summary

The characteristics of our current society and the roles assigned to teachers suggest the need for more comprehensive programs of teacher education. Four-year teacher education programs have not produced teachers who can guide students to a level of achievement expected and needed by our society. The research literature has established a knowledge base for teacher education, including breadth in the liberal arts and depth in teaching fields and field experiences, that cannot be represented adequately in a four-year program.

If the public really wants school reform to succeed in establishing higher levels of student achievement and the basis for improved life-styles for all of our citizens, then they must support changes in the education of the classroom teacher. Our children deserve no less; our society can prosper with no less.

References

American Association of Colleges for Teacher Education (AACTE). *Educating a Profession: Extended Programs for Teacher Education.* Washington, D.C.: AACTE, 1976.

American Association of Colleges for Teacher Education (AACTE). *Educating a Profession: Profile of a Beginning Teacher.* Washington, D.C.: AACTE, 1983.

Association of American Colleges (AAC). *Project on Redefining the Meaning and Purpose of Baccalaureate Degrees.* Washington, D.C.: AAC, 1985.

Berliner, D. C. "Making the Right Changes in Preservice Teacher Education." *Phi Delta Kappan,* 1984, 66 (2), 94-96.

Cremin, L. A. "The Education of the Educating Professions." Nineteenth Annual Charles W. Hunt Lecture. Washington, D.C.: American Association of Colleges for Teacher Education, 1977.

Gage, N. L. *The Scientific Basis for the Art of Teaching:* New York: Teachers College Press, 1978.

Gage, N. L. "What Do We Know About Teaching Effectiveness." *Phi Delta Kappan,* 1984, 66 (2), 87-93.

Galambos, E. C. *Teacher Preparation: The Anatomy of a College Degree.* Atlanta: Southern Regional Education Board, 1985.

Gallegos, A. "The Dilemma of Extended Programs." *Journal of Teacher Education,* 1981, 32 (6), 4-6.

Gideonse, H. "The Necessary Revolution in Teacher Education." *Phi Delta Kappan,* 1982, 64, (18), 15-18.

Howsam, R. B., Corrigan, D. C., Denmark, G. W., and Nash, R. J. *Educating a Profession*. Washington, D.C.: American Association of Colleges for Teacher Education, 1976.

National Association of State Universities and Land-Grant Colleges (NASULGC). *Report of the Executive Committee of the Academic Affairs Council on Elementary and Secondary Education*. Washington, D.C.: NASULGC, 1984.

National Institute of Education (NIE). *Involvement in Learning: Realizing the Potential of American Higher Education*. Washington, D.C.: NIE, 1984.

Reynolds, M. C. (Ed.). *A Common Body of Practice for Teachers: The Challenge of Public Law 94-142 to Teacher Education*. Washington, D.C.: American Association of Colleges for Teacher Education, 1980.

Sharp, B. L. (Ed.). *Dean's Grant Projects: Challenge and Change in Teacher Education*. Minneapolis: National Support System Project, 1982.

Smith, B. O. *A Design for a School of Pedagogy*. Washington, D.C.: U.S. Department of Education, 1980a.

Smith, B. O. "Now Is the Time to Advance Pedagogical Education." *Educational Theory*, 1980b, *30* (3), 177-183.

Smith, D. C. (Ed.). *Essential Knowledge for Beginning Educators*. Washington, D.C.: American Association of Colleges for Teacher Education, 1983.

Dale P. Scannell is dean, College of Education, University of Maryland–College Park.

The cost of extending teacher education to include a fifth year would be $6 billion annually, and there is no evidence that extended programs produce more effective teachers.

The Risks and Inadequacy of Extended Programs

Willis D. Hawley

The five-year teacher preparation movement, which encompasses many programmatic variations, has powerful proponents. Among them are a special task force of the American Association of Colleges for Teacher Education (AACTE) and the majority of the members of the National Commission for Excellence in Teacher Education. The deans of about two dozen schools of education at major universities, who call themselves The Holmes Group, would require five years of college *and* an internship for entry into teaching. Many leading schools of education (Chicago, Stanford, Teachers College, Columbia, and the Universities of Kansas and Florida) now offer teacher training only at the postbaccalaureate level. Some other schools of education are actively involved in the development of five-year programs. California requires all teachers to complete a postbaccalaureate year of teacher preparation before being fully certified.

Much of the debate over four- versus five-year teacher preparation programs consists of unsubstantiated claims and assumptions (*Journal of Teacher Education,* 1981). It is time to subject the proposals to more analysis about the costs and consequences of these programs than proponents have offered so far. If the ultimate goal of teacher education reform is to enhance the education of elementary and secondary school students, the problem faced by government and higher education policy makers who are considering extended programs is how to decide whether such an investment of money and energy is the most cost-effective strategy for enhancing student learning.

One reason that extended programs have not been subjected to more criticism is that there are so many variations. Extended programs in this chapter are considered to be any that *require* students to take a minimum of five years of *college-based* coursework (including practice teaching) before they are allowed to teach at full salary.

The Risks of Mandating Extended Programs

There are two risks in requiring all teacher candidates to complete extended programs: (1) The costs of becoming a teacher would increase, and, without *significant* improvements in teacher compensation and working conditions, the quality and quantity of candidates in the applicant pool would decline; and (2) the costs of implementing extended programs would deny resources to other more productive educational reforms.

The costs of a five-year teacher preparation program to *individuals* are of two types. First, there is the cost of tuition and fees, which in 1985 is estimated at about $1,400 per year at a four-year public institution. (Room and board costs are assumed to be constant for college graduates still in school and those teaching.) The cost to students of adding a fifth year at private colleges and universities is four to five times this amount.

A second cost to individuals is forgone earnings. In 1985–1986, first year teachers earned salaries and fringe benefits worth about $18,000. (This assumes fringe benefits worth about 20 percent of a $15,000 salary.) Thus, a fifth year of college required prior to entry into the profession increases the overall cost of becoming a teacher at a public college or university by $19,400 for the average individual (the cost of a lost year of teaching plus a year's tuition). The costs would be much higher for students attending private colleges.

These are very substantial additions to the costs individuals currently incur to become a teacher—much higher than alluded to by advocates of five-year programs (AACTE, 1983). These advocates seldom count forgone earnings, and they often argue that over time the five-year teacher will make up the amount by earning higher salaries. They assert that the fifth year of study will qualify individuals for a higher salary than having only a bachelor's degree, so the money forgone will be quickly earned back. However, typically, a master's degree would only add $1,500 to a teacher's annual earnings. (While not all five-year programs lead to a master's degree [AACTE, 1983], it is assumed here that they would do so.)

If the four-year teacher begins a master's program in the second year of service and completes the degree in three years by going to school part-time, the four-year teacher would catch up with the five-year teacher over a period of time where the income advantage of the five-year teacher would total about $6,000 (in 1985-1986 dollars). But the five-year teacher "lost" more than $18,000 in forgone earnings. Thus, other things being equal, the five-year teacher will never earn in his or her lifetime what the four-year teacher will earn, even if the four-year teacher pays $1,500 in tuition while pursuing the master's degree. (These estimates do not include the considerable cost of a loan if the individual has to borrow money to pursue a fifth year of study. The cost to the individual is the same whether or not a loan is taken out, since the money would otherwise be invested.)

Suggestions that some of the $19,400 of additional costs for becoming a teacher can be amortized over time may not be persuasive to teacher candidates, *many* of whom are not sure they want to teach for a very long time. Moreover, if one cannot forgo the $19,400 one would earn teaching, the idea that there is a reasonable return on investment (an incorrect assumption in any case) is irrelevant. Historically, teaching has drawn its candidates from those least able to make such an investment.

In summary, increasing the costs of becoming a teacher reduces the attractiveness of the profession unless these costs are offset by intrinsic and extrinsic benefits not now available. Those who will drop out of the pool will be those who are brightest, have the best interpersonal skills, are the most imaginative, and thus have broader career options. This proposition is a fundamental assumption made by labor economists and is akin to the idea that the quality of our teachers cannot be improved without raising teachers' salaries significantly (an argument often made by advocates of extended programs). There are those who argue that since teachers are not motivated by money, they will not take these new costs into account. But the market is now in equilibrium. That is, those students whose altruism leads them to discount economic benefits have been attracted. If the economic costs are raised, the intrinsic rewards from teaching will have to be raised, or a decline in the quality and quantity of teacher candidates will result. Extended programs do not alter the intrinsic rewards of teaching unless they alter significantly the occupational prestige enjoyed by teachers.

There are noneconomic factors, too, that would decrease the quality and quantity of those entering teaching if undergraduate preparation programs are eliminated. National studies demonstrate that college students become increasingly materialistic and concerned with their own welfare, and therefore less likely to consider teaching, as they progress through the undergraduate program. Undergraduate teacher education programs can attract idealistic students by providing them with opportunities to experience the intrinsic rewards of teaching, to have the support of like-minded peers, and to be socialized by their professors. Ralph Tyler (1985) draws attention to the findings of the Commission on Teacher Education, which concluded in its 1944 report that attracting altruistic and able young people to teaching was enhanced significantly by providing freshmen and sophomores the opportunity to be involved in schools from the time they entered college.

Also, by providing potential teachers with early field experiences, undergraduates who are not really interested in or suited for teaching may readjust career plans, usually without any substantial loss of earned credits. For students who change their plans, it is much harder to salvage credits earned at the graduate level, where prospective teachers might encounter their first field experiences in the extended programs.

A likely consequence of eliminating undergraduate teacher certification is a substantial reduction in the role now played by liberal arts colleges in the preparation of teachers. The ability of such schools to offer a full and up-to-date curriculum in education varies widely. But it is virtually certain it will be even more difficult to attract young teachers educated at selective and high-quality colleges such as Reed, Swarthmore, Dartmouth, and Oberlin if such students will have to complete five versus four years of teacher education. The same point seems applicable to universities that do not have schools of education but that now offer programs of undergraduate teacher certification. Such universities include Emory, Rice, Washington (St. Louis), and Tulane. This means that the role played by private colleges and universities in the education of the nation's teachers will decline. Aside from the practical consequences of losing such high-status colleges and universities from the teacher education business, the symbolic importance of their involvement in the preparation of teachers should not be overlooked. It is not inconsequential that Harvard is returning to the business of undergraduate teacher preparation, even though very few teachers will be Harvard graduates.

The Economic Costs of Extended Programs

Some advocates of extended teacher preparation are aware that such programs are likely to have a negative effect on the size and quality of the teaching force. Thus, some would-be reformers suggest governmental subsidies for extended programs. How much would it cost to *maintain* the quality of the teacher candidate pool? Conventional economic analysis suggests the need to offset the added costs of entry to retain the same quality of entrant (Manski, 1985). On the basis of the National Center for Education Statistics estimate that as many as 200,000 new teachers will be needed annually in the late 1980s (Plisko and Stern, 1985), the annual costs to taxpayers of subsidies for extended programs could be close to $4 billion!

If subsidies are paid by states, this will constrain the mobility of teachers. Current financial incentives for math and science teachers require the beneficiaries to teach within their states to repay loans. Reduced competition for teachers across state lines will reduce pressure for increasing their salaries.

Regardless of whether government subsidies are available, extended programs will increase costs to taxpayers. Requiring students to attend college for five instead of four years will add 25 percent in costs to taxpayers, to be provided in courses, facilities, and student services. In the short run, some of these costs will be offset by underutilized resources. In the long run, however, savings in the public's cost for higher education that could be recovered owing to the decline in the college-age population would be lost in fifth year teacher education costs.

The average publicly subsidized cost of one year of college for each of the students who annually graduate from teacher education programs is about $10,000. This represents the annual per student expenditure for public four-year colleges (Plisko, 1984) minus average tuition in public universities. The subsidized cost for private education is about the same, although most of the funds do not come *directly* from public revenues. Taking into account the role of private institutions and the fact that many teachers ultimately get a master's degree, the additional higher education resources would cost taxpayers about $1 billion more than if teachers entered the profession after four years of college. (This assumes that 75 percent of the teachers would be educated in public institutions and that some of the added cost of full-time students would be reduced by that for part-time students [who do not usually add much to overhead costs]. If, as is likely, students shift from private to public institutions, the taxpayers' costs would rise another $250 million.) If the fifth year results in a master's degree, then taxpayers would also pay higher salaries for teachers, and this would add close to one billion dollars to the costs of extended programs. (The master's degree teacher would earn $1,500 more each year than the four-year teacher until the four-year teacher also earned the advanced degree four years later. During that time in any given year, the master's differential is being paid to the master's entrants in each of the four years. Assuming an attrition rate of 33 percent over the four years, the cost would be $4,000 for 200,000 teachers or $800,000.)

Altogether, the annual cost of implementing extended teacher preparation programs nationwide approximates $6 billion. This would comprise a large share of the estimated $12 billion spent nationwide on new directions for education in 1984–1985. Should society make that kind of additional investment in teacher education rather than increase teacher salaries, improve skills of those already teaching, reduce class size for low achieving children, or provide early childhood education for the disadvantaged?

Will Extended Programs Improve the Quality of Teaching?

In view of the considerable costs of extended programs, a persuasive case should be presented by advocates that the change will significantly improve the quality of teaching. They should make the following assumptions about extended programs: (1) The teaching profession will gain status, and this will increase salaries and the attractions of teaching to able students; (2) Students will learn more about teaching in extended programs; (3) Teachers trained in extended programs will be better trained in subject fields; (4) Taking more liberal arts courses will make students better teachers; and (5) What students learn in college about teaching will be reflected in their performance on the job.

Assumption 1: The Teaching Profession Will Become More Attractive. Will an additional year of schooling increase teachers' salaries and the status of teaching? Generally, earnings and educational attainment are not closely related once college graduation is assured, especially for women. Teacher salaries declined in the 1970s relative to other occupations despite increasing proportions of teachers with master's degrees. Also, it is unlikely that the public will pay substantial bonuses for master's degrees if it has already been called on to finance an extended teachers' program. Moreover, public funds to implement extended programs may diminish the resources available for whatever general teacher salary increases might otherwise have ensued.

Does more required education lead to a higher status for a given profession? To be sure, advanced education is correlated with occupational prestige. But many jobs (for example, engineers, journalists, and many business people) require no more than a college degree for entry and yet have higher status than teaching. Education is only one component of occupational prestige (Treiman, 1977), and reflects, in part, perceptions of higher education as a measure of intellectual ability. One reason teachers do not have higher status is that there are so many of them. Ten percent of all college graduates are needed annually to staff the schools; more people are inducted into teaching annually than enter the armed forces.

Teachers' salaries in California, the one state that requires completion of a fifth year of college for full certification, have been similar to those in many nonsouthern states for several years. In 1985-1986, beginning teacher salaries in California rose to $18,500—above the national average. But to attribute this increase to a requirement that was established more than a decade ago would be wrong. It seems more likely that the recent increase (which is not so remarkable in view of the cost of living there) in California teachers' salaries reflects concern about the quality and quantity of those who have chosen to teach. Many cities in California cannot fill teacher positions, and teaching candidates rank near the bottom of thirty occupations with respect to measures of verbal and quantitative abilities (Kerchner, 1983.)

Assumption 2: Students Will Learn More About How to Teach. A major argument for fifth year programs is, of course, that teachers so educated will know more about teaching. They will take more professional coursework, and it will be at a more sophisticated and demanding level. However, one-year postbaccalaureate certification programs limit students to fewer education courses than they might take in most undergraduate programs. If teachers' *initial* training in extended programs resulted in a master's degree, the total amount of *formal* professional education the typical career teacher receives probably would be less than it is now. Currently, the typical high school teacher certified with a baccalaureate degree will have completed sixty semester units of professional coursework by the time he or she earns a master's degree. The person who receives a master's degree on completion of a one-year postbaccalaureate program will take half this much coursework. This argument will not be persuasive to those who discount the value of professional education, but these are presumably not among the advocates of five-year programs.

It might be argued that the graduate courses in extended programs will be more intellectually demanding and thus students will learn more about how to teach. Graduate courses in education, however, are not typically described as intellectually demanding, and they are not known as being more rigorous than undergraduate courses. Why should they be? They will be taught by the same faculty. Being twenty-two years old instead of twenty or twenty-one does not make students better learners. While a year of maturation is not likely to increase individuals' cognitive capabilities, persons pursuing a master's degree or a fifth year of study are likely to be more productive learners once they have actually taught in schools and classrooms, because they can then use their experience to frame questions and organize information. Good teaching involves an enormously complex and demanding set of intellectual tasks. Learning how to perform those tasks is likely to be easier if teachers have experienced what the process of teaching actually involves.

Assumption 3: Teachers Will Be Better Trained in Their Subject Field. Extended programs that require undergraduate education courses will not open up much space in the curriculum for subject matter courses. To the extent that they do, or that postbaccalaureate-only programs do free up time for subject matter courses, future elementary teachers will be able to take more math, science, English, or social studies courses. But extended programs would have little impact on the number of courses in their subject field for secondary teachers. Most education schools now require secondary teacher candidates to complete a disciplinary major or the equivalent. Of course, the content of the courses prospective teachers take is more important than the numbers, but this point is not relevant to the debate about the length of preservice teacher education. Moreover, there is reason to believe that additional coursework or a teacher's greater-than-average knowledge of a subject does not contribute to effective teaching, except in advanced courses (Druva and Anderson, 1983). This last point seems counterintuitive, but it may suggest that what matters is not how many courses one has had or how well one has done in them, but whether one understands fundamental principles and the structure of the discipline or body of knowledge involved (see Leinhardt and Smith, 1985).

Assumption 4: More Liberal Arts Courses Will Make Students More Effective Teachers. Some advocates of extended programs, particularly those who argue that teacher preparation programs should begin after undergraduate education has been completed, believe that this reform will make teachers better educated and thus more effective.

If no increases in the number of education courses accompanied the implementation of extended programs, five years of college for teacher preparation would permit students to take eight to ten electives in lieu of education courses at the undergraduate level. There is, however, absolutely no evidence that such a change would make students better teachers. Whether more liberal arts courses would improve teaching depends on the difference between the intellectual content of the electives and the education courses a student takes. No doubt there are education courses that are undemanding and devoid of theory and methods of inquiry that characterize the *best* of liberal arts courses, but many students choose these courses on the basis of how undemanding they are (Galambos and others, 1985).

If it is true that many liberal arts courses are more rigorous than many education courses, then there is a need to change the content of education courses. The well-traveled path to academic rigor is through tougher grading policies. Other more fundamental strategies include the incorporation of new research and significant theory in the curriculum, the insistence that students be held to high performance expectations, and attention to the development of student skills of critical inquiry and written expression.

Assumption 5: Students' College Experiences Will Be Reflected in Their Performance on the Job. This argument for extended programs is that there is now more knowledge about how to teach effectively than ever before, and that teachers should have this information and be able to use it before they enter the classroom. This argument assumes that what teacher candidates learn before they become teachers is often put to good use in the classroom. However, recent research clearly demonstrates that much of what teachers learn in the preservice stage of their career is undone or substantially mitigated during the first year or two of teaching and, perhaps, by the practice teaching experience (Evertson and others, 1985). Increasing the amount of information and skills teachers learn in college is an inefficient and, perhaps, futile strategy unless ways are devised to enhance the ability of teachers to put into practice what they have previously learned. The Holmes Group has recognized this problem and advocates intensively supervised internships. These, however, when added to the extended program, further increase the costs of entry for individuals or to the public for preparing new teachers.

Conclusion

The possibility that extended programs will reduce the quality and quantity of teachers is high, and the likelihood that these programs will improve teacher performance is not great. This does not mean that the profession should not experiment with extended programs, but it does mean that such *trials* should be carefully evaluated. Furthermore, if the risks of extended programs seem high and the benefits uncertain, other strategies for improving teacher education should be explored more aggressively than they have been. Two such alternatives are the reform of undergraduate programs and postbaccalaureate internships. These two strategies would complement each other, and, taken together, would almost certainly be more cost effective than extended programs.

Current knowledge about teacher effectiveness is incomplete and will inevitably change. Therefore the training of a teacher must be seen as the beginning of a career that is characterized by recurrent opportunities for professional growth, including graduate school. Prospective teachers must be skilled at learning and applying new information to the solution of the complex and varied problems they confront. Their ability to learn on the job would be facilitated if teachers were better able to manage their classrooms and the teaching/learning process, use theory as a tool for learning and inventing, and engage in systematic inquiry that would help them resolve the dilemmas and uncertainties with which they must inevitably deal. It follows that programs for the education of teachers should give more emphasis to these areas than they currently do (see Joyce and Cliff, 1984).

An absolutely essential part of any teacher education reform program is the provision to teachers of significant support as they make the transition from college to independent classroom teaching. Depending on how such support may be provided, it would be feasible to transfer practice teaching and possibly specific methods courses out of the undergraduate curriculum (or graduate program, for that matter) and make these part of the induction process. The suggestion by Schlechty (see Chapter Four) that academies be established for training teachers represents a promising alternative and one for which there is growing political support.

The case for extended programs rests on precarious analogies to other professions that are very differently organized and financially supported and on the expert judgment of teacher educators from large universities. The truth is that relatively little is known about how to educate effective teachers. There is almost no research on the effectiveness of alternative ways of educating teachers. Before initiating major systemwide changes in the requirements students must meet to teach, it would be prudent to experiment with different strategies and curricula and then evaluate their relative effectiveness. This will require collaboration among state education departments, colleges and departments of education, and school systems. It is ironic that a knowledge-based industry like education has been so little interested in using research to determine how better to perform its function.

At a time when there is so much doubt about the usefulness of teacher education, there is a need for deregulation, for innovation, and most important, for evaluation of how the alternatives affect student learning in the schools. There are surely better ways to educate teachers than are now generally in use. But it is not probable that there is one best way, and perhaps there never will be.

References

American Association of Colleges for Teacher Education (AACTE). *Educating a Profession: Extended Programs for Teacher Education.* Washington, D.C.: AACTE, 1976.

Druva, C. A., and Anderson, R. D. "Science Teacher Characteristics by Teacher Behavior and by Student Outcome: A Meta-Analysis of Research." *Journal of Research in Science Teaching,* 1983, *20* (5), 467-479.

Evertson, C., Hawley, W. D., and Zlotnik, M. "Making a Difference in Educational Quality Through Teacher Education." *Journal of Teacher Education,* 1985, *36,* 2-12.

Galambos, E. C., Cornett, L. M., and Spitler, H. D. *An Analysis of Transcripts of Teachers and Arts and Science Graduates.* Atlanta: Southern Regional Education Board, 1985.

Journal of Teacher Education (Entire issue deals with four- versus five-year teacher education programs.) 1981, *32.*

Joyce, B., and Cliff, R. "The Phoenix Agenda: Essential Reform in Teacher Education." *Educational Research,* 1984, *13* (4), 5-18.

Kerchner, C. T. *Flood Times and Aging Swimmers: An Exploration into the Supply and Demand for Teachers.* Claremont, Calif.: Claremont Graduate School, 1983.

Leinhardt, G., and Smith, D. "Expertise in Mathematics Instruction, Subject Matter Knowledge." *Journal of Educational Psychology,* 1985, *77,* 241-271.

Manski, C. *Academic Ability, Earnings, and the Decision to Become a Teacher: Evidence from the National Longitudinal Study of the High School Class of 1972.* (Working paper no. 1539). Cambridge, Mass.: National Bureau of Economic Research, 1985.

Plisko, V. W. *The Condition of Education: 1984 Edition.* Washington, D.C.: U.S. Government Printing Office, 1984.

Treiman, D. J. *Occupation Prestige in Comparative Perspective.* New York: Academic Press, 1977.

Tyler, R. "What We've Learned from Past Studies of Teacher Education." *Phi Delta Kappan,* 1985, *66,* 682-684.

Willis D. Hawley is dean of Peabody College, Vanderbilt University, Nashville, Tennessee.

A new type of teacher education organization is needed that is outside the public schools, outside the university, and outside the teachers' organizations. Such an organization might be called the Academy for Excellence in Teaching and Educational Leadership.

Public School and Teacher Education Reform: A Proposal for Shared Action

Phillip C. Schlechty, Betty Lou Whitford

The purpose of this chapter is to link reforms in the public schools and in teacher education. Teacher education cannot be much improved until institutions of higher education redirect their energies in the field of teacher education and until public schools play a more central role in teacher education than is now the case. This is not to suggest that schools of education should be closed or that teacher training should simply be turned over to public schools. Rather, universities and schools of education should continue to play a central role in the preparation of teachers. However, if teacher education is to survive, the functions of higher education in the education of teachers must be redefined.

The primary strength of institutions of higher education is the capacity of these institutions to develop students' abilities to study important subjects in disciplined and systematic ways. It is important for prospective teachers to study those subjects they will teach. In addition, there is another subject that prospective teachers must master—the subject of education. Therefore, institutions of higher education have an obligation to ensure that prospective teachers develop and demonstrate the capacity to study education-related subjects (such as, the research on effective teaching and effective schools, child development, and so on) and a mastery of the subjects to be taught.

There is, however, a fundamental difference between developing the ability to study subjects and developing the ability to teach. Institutions of higher education are skilled at teaching people how to study subjects. However, they are not particularly adept (in any field) at teaching people how to perform on the job. For example, IBM provides a management training program for employees, law firms provide apprenticeships for graduate lawyers, and teaching hospitals prepare future physicians. Institutions of higher education can and should supply elementary and secondary teachers who have a demonstrated capacity to study education. But teachers, like managers, lawyers, and physicians, learn their craft where the craft is practiced. Teachers learn to teach in schools; this will remain true regardless of the curriculum reforms that take place in teacher education or the quality of the teacher education curriculum.

There are, of course, those who argue that there is little substantive knowledge about teaching and school management and that what passes for knowledge in the teacher education curriculum is intellectually vacuous and largely irrelevant. One need not be an apologist for present modes of teacher education to reject this argument. There is, in fact, a growing body of research, systematic theory, and disciplined lore that can and should inform the practices of teachers and school leaders. The problem is that, as the teacher education enterprise is currently organized, there is no formal organizational link between those who study teaching and school leadership and the schools. As long as teacher educators and teacher education researchers are in a different accountability and status system than those of schools, it is unlikely that such an organizational linkage will occur.

If the knowledge that teachers and school administrators need is to be transmitted to them in ways that will inform practice, then the way public schools and institutions of higher education are related to each other must be fundamentally restructured, especially in the field of teacher and administrator preparation. Dreeben (1970) put the matter well when he wrote:

> Although there is much to be said for showing concern about the competence of teachers, the question of competence may be more fully understood in terms of the occupational characteristics of teaching rather than in terms of the curriculum of teacher training institutions. . . . Problems of competence grow out of the relationship among schools of education, universities, and school systems; between training institutions and prevailing career patterns; and from the way these institutions shape the occupation and its members [p. 4].

The Current Scene

As indicated, one need not disparage professional education courses or teacher educators to observe that Waller's (1932) assertion of over fifty years ago is true: "teachers still learn to teach by teaching" (p. 1). Research since Waller's time only serves to reinforce this assertion. The social context within which instruction occurs and the social processes by which knowledge is transmitted shape, mold, and sometimes redirect the intended outcomes. Thus, concentrating on the knowledge and skills that are to be transmitted without attending to the social context in which instruction occurs is likely to lead to dysfunctional outcomes.

As things stand now, teacher educators exhort students to acknowledge the primacy of theory as a source of direction for practice; yet most teacher educators acknowledge that there continues to be a schism between educational theory and educational practice. Rather than giving theory a place of primacy in their system of values, many teachers disdain theory and find it useless. As Waller (1932) observed:

> Both the theory and practice of education have suffered from an overattention to what ought to be and its correlative tendency to disregard what is. When theory is not based on existing practice, a great hiatus appears between theory and practice, and the consequence is that the progressiveness of theory does not affect the conservatism of practice [p. 192].

> A central point of the teacher's training . . . should be the attempt to give him insight into the nature of the social reality that is the school. This is what teachers usually learn in the hard school of experience and by those rules of thumb that experience gives; and this is another reason for the conservatism of educational practice. Prospective teachers learn all the new educational theories while they are in school, but they must learn how to teach from horny-handed men who have been teaching a long time. But if theory is ever really to be translated into practice, theorists must learn to follow it through the social dynamics of the classroom. Only so can experience be fruitful in the understanding that will make possible a change of things that are [p. 459].

Many teacher educators are sympathetic to the view that teacher education should be more field oriented and that professors of education should "practice what they preach, exemplify what they explicate" (Howsam and others, 1975). There is reason to believe, however, that such exhortations, even if acted on, would yield little that is positive. For example, it can be convincingly argued that university-based professors and public school teachers are not even in the same occupational group (see Lortie, 1975). University professors are expected and required to engage in research. They are rewarded if they do so and are punished if they do not. In the typical public school, there are few rewards for doing research and no punishments for failing to engage in such activities. Five classes a day, five days a week seem quite enough to most teachers.

In recent years, there have been numerous projects that have clearly demonstrated that some teachers can engage in meaningful research while carrying on regular classroom instruction (see, for example, Nixon, 1981; Biles and others, 1983; Hovda and Kyle, 1983; Tikunoff and Mergendoller, 1983). Furthermore, there is substantial evidence that by engaging in research, teachers not only contribute some new knowledge about teaching, but they also are more likely to systematically improve their own practice. Unfortunately, as Whitford (1984) has observed, without fundamental restructuring of the job of teaching and without fundamental redesign of the reward and status systems of schools, such efforts are not likely to be systematically pursued by many teachers as a normal activity. Furthermore, those teachers who do pursue such activity are likely to abandon research simply because the system does not provide them continuing encouragement and support.

To suggest that a college professor can teach in a way that public school teachers can reasonably be expected to emulate implies that conditions in the college classroom are equivalent or at least roughly comparable to conditions in the public school. Unfortunately, the problems of motivation, direction, and control are not the same for a seventh-grade class and for a college class. There are, in addition, many other fundamental differences between campus conditions and those in public schools (such as, class loads, time for planning, personal reflection, conferences, conversations with colleagues, and so on).

If teacher educators are to serve as effective models for classroom teachers (and such models are needed), they must find ways to demonstrate their competence under classroom conditions that are recognizable and understood by the typical teachers. This can be accomplished only if teacher educators are placed in a position where a part of their regular assignment includes responsibility for the daily instruction of *some* students in an existing school system.

The Need for a New Approach

The aim of professional preparation is to develop the knowledge, skills, and abilities needed for the complex job of teaching. The goal is also to develop and maintain a commitment to the occupational group and to the high performance standards of that group. In addition, professional education must foster attitudes, beliefs, and values that are supportive of high quality performance even under adverse conditions and encourage interdependent action among mutually supportive colleagues. Thus, professional training programs must foster peer criticism, peer review, and peer evaluation.

To accomplish such a complex and comprehensive task, a variety of functions not commonly associated with on-the-job training or formal programs of instruction must be coordinated and managed. For example, professional training programs must give systematic attention to recruitment and socialization processes as well as to those processes related directly to the development of knowledge and skills. Professional training programs must be concerned with how well the student does things as well as with what understanding a student has of what he or she does.

What is needed, therefore, is a mechanism for bringing together in a single agency those functions of knowledge generation and codification, recruitment and selection, knowledge transmission, socialization, and evaluation. Otherwise, the conditions described by Clark and Marker (1975) will be perpetuated: "In this framework of organized irresponsibility, there is not only endless opportunity to avoid accountability but a rational posture that is available to each partner in the enterprise to justify avoidance" (pp. 75-76).

A Proposal for Change

There are few, if any, cases in which institutional arrangements have undergone fundamental restructuring without those in the existing power structure having first perceived that without such change, the central goals of the organization would be threatened. Furthermore, there are few instances in which radical change has occurred in an organization without a group that has developed sufficient power and authority to compel the change. (The willingness of the United Automobile Workers to renegotiate traditional power and authority arrangements relative to the new General Motors Saturn plant is clearly a response to the emerging power threat from outside organizations, in this case foreign automakers.)

Institutional changes are resisted primarily because they cause shifts in the existing power structure. Those who occupy power positions are likely to seek to preserve the structure, since it is in their self-interest to do so. Furthermore, the power available to insiders in an organization is more likely to be legitimately used to maintain the system than to change it. Indeed, insiders who use their power for change without support from the outside are likely to receive sanctions by those above them and those below them in the organization.

Thus, it is unlikely that, as insiders, teacher educators, teachers, or school administrators can or will bring about the changes that are needed to further the ends of professional education for teachers. What is needed is a mechanism where change-oriented teachers, teacher educators, and public school administrators can come together as outsiders (outside the present teacher education and public school establishment) and organize for change. What is needed is the creation of a new type of teacher education organization that has the ability to bring together in a single place those who can provide the basic functions of knowledge generation and codification, recruitment and selection, occupational socialization, training, and evaluation. This organization must be able to command the loyalties of all who participate so that the nonprofessional interests of universities, public schools, and teachers' organizations are excluded from the decision-making structure of the new organization. What is needed, in brief, is an organization that is outside the public schools, universities, and teachers' organizations and which has sufficient power and authority to compel these organizations' respect and accord on matters of teacher education. This new organization could then become a central point in a change system that could encourage (perhaps even enforce) the kinds of changes required for professionalized teacher education. Such an organization might be called the Academy for Excellence in Teaching and Educational Leadership.

The training mission of this academy would be directed toward preparing new teachers and providing continuing education for those already in the field. The primary research mission would describe and analyze teaching in classroom settings. Attention would, of course, be given to nonclassroom instruction, but it seems likely that the professional educator's primary base of operation will continue to be a classroom of twenty-five or more children. Thus, research and theory development relevant to the technology of teaching would be conducted in such settings.

The relationship between an academy and a public school system would be symbiotic, not parasitic. Academies could be established within existing school systems or consortia of small systems; however, the administrative and staff structures of the local education agency (LEA) and the academy should be distinguishable and at the same time intermeshed, much like the relationship between a teaching hospital staff and a medical school faculty. For example, many of the academy's faculty might carry out some routine functions for the local school system, such as regularly teaching one or more classes. In performing this function, academy staff would be directly accountable to the administration of the local school system. Similarly, many of the local school staff might serve functions that would be supervised by the faculty of the academy, and these staff members would be accountable to the administrative structure of the academy. For example, the role of mentor for new teachers could be a role specifically assigned to the staff of the academy.

The relationship between the academy and affiliated institutions of higher education would also be symbiotic. The training program developed by academies would require some campus-based activities—especially in the liberal arts and in selected preprofessional education courses. Some of the latter courses might be taken as part of a baccalaureate program or as part of a master's degree program and used as a prerequisite for employment in the affiliated public schools or for entry into academy training programs. There is clearly a legitimate place for the study of education in the preparation of teachers, just as there is a place for the liberal arts and sciences. However, the study of education has approximately the same relationship to the professional preparation of teachers as the study of anatomy has to the preparation of physicians.

Another point of contact between the academy and higher education institutions would be in the preparation of future staff members for the academy and in the preparation of researchers. The university campus is the appropriate location for the substantive preparation of educational researchers. Thus, the academy would be dependent on colleges and universities to provide appropriately prepared teacher educators and researchers. In return, the staff of the academy would work with faculty from affiliated colleges and universities to create appropriate practicum experiences for educational researchers and teacher educators and would provide a supportive environment for internships and research activity.

It should be emphasized, however, that the academy would not be the creature of a university or a school of education any more than it would be the creature of a teachers' organization or a local education agency. Indeed, one of the bases for university affiliation with such an academy should be that the university would agree to provide an appropriate preprofessional baccalaureate program as well as to offer supportive environments for the advanced preparation of researchers and teacher educators.

Basically, then, the function of the university with regard to the academy would be to provide appropriate preprofessional preparation in the liberal arts and in the study of education. For example, courses based on the research in effective teaching and effective schools could be offered to pre-teacher training students. Other courses that might be offered would be logic of inquiry, psychometrics, ethics, and aesthetics.

Although the university would lose control over the clinical components of teacher education, the emergence of the academy would provide an entirely new and expanded market for university graduates as well as useful sites for research and experimentation. For example, there would be an expanded market for teacher educators to staff the new academies as well as a market for a new breed of researchers.

The relationship between the academy and the local teachers' association would be similar to the academy's relationship with the local education agency. Many, yet not all, of the staff of the academy would be members of the local teachers' association. The local teachers' association would certainly participate in the governance of the academy (as would the local education agency and affiliated institutions of higher education). However, the teachers' association would not have dominant control.

Like universities and local school administrators, teachers' organizations have interests in teacher education that are both incompatible with and supportive of professionalization. Therefore, a system of governance must be established that represents the professional interests of each of these groups or agencies and acts against those interests that hinder or jeopardize professionalism. The creation of such governance structures will be a difficult and politically sensitive task, but it must be dealt with if educational quality is to be maintained and improved.

Some Critical Concerns

There are many factors that must be taken into account in any plan to create an organization such as the academy. Among the more critical of these are:

1. Since the academy concept is necessarily threatening to many who are now in the teacher education establishment, some means must be found to reduce this threat to a tolerable level and thereby avoid outright resistance to the academy concept. If appropriate funding could be assured, the academy would offer affiliated local institutions of higher education inducements, such as (a) *paid* research leaves to professors as visiting research scholars, (b) pay to doctoral students to conduct (or assist the academy staff in conducting) research that is sponsored by the academy, and (c) contracts to provide appropriate pre-entry courses for promising candidates who have not yet shown that they are students of education (for instance, liberal arts majors and education majors from traditional teacher education programs).

2. The academy would be especially threatening to some building level administrators and classroom teachers, especially those who are bureaucratically oriented or who view teaching as a job rather than as a professional career. There is no foolproof means of offsetting this threat, but the academy staff could encourage administrators and teachers to develop the skills and competency necessary to fill the roles suggested by the differentiated career structure of the academy (such as, the teacher as mentor, the principal as teacher educator). Indeed, during the first several years of its existence, an academy might center activities on intensive inservice programs for local teachers and administrators aimed at qualifying them for such roles.

3. Changing the role structure of the school system requires that the reward structure also be changed. At a minimum, it requires that those who are qualified to advance to staff status in the academy receive a salary

commensurate with their training and skill. Although pay at the level of beginning physicians is probably unrealistic, a pay scale equivalent to that enjoyed by graduate engineers and architects does not seem out of line. In addition, generous provision for paid attendance at professional meetings and conferences should be considered along with the provision of appropriate secretarial and office support.

4. The academy would need to have considerable control over establishing criteria for admission and the ability to link admission directly to employment prospects within the affiliated school site. Thus, clear agreements among the local school board, the teachers' association, and the academy staff would have to be negotiated. To the extent possible, provisions should be made for potential attrition (trainees who for one reason or another select to pursue careers in other school systems) as well as for continued employment.

5. Realistic standards for evaluation would need to be established. Such evaluation should begin with evidence that teachers have been affected by the program and should culminate with evidence concerning the impact of their teaching on student learning. However, efforts to tie measures of success immediately to measurable student learning outcomes should be resisted, for such evaluations are likely to lead to goal displacement and to cosmetic change rather than long-term systematic change.

The Issues of Feasibility

The changes suggested in this chapter will not be easy to implement. Even if policymakers and funding agencies are willing to approach educational reform on a long-term basis, what will it take to implement the suggested changes? There are at least four necessary courses of action.

1. Local school systems and teachers' organizations must commit themselves to making teacher education as much a part of public education as is the education of children. This commitment will of necessity require that the school system, or some part of it, be turned into the educational equivalent of a teaching hospital.

2. Long-term, developmental funding will be needed, without narrow accountability measures, at least in the beginning. (It is significant that the reform in medical education during the late nineteenth and early twentieth centuries gained much of its impetus from the development of a long-term plan for change at Johns Hopkins University that was supported by a generous endowment from a private source. Staff for the Johns Hopkins Medical School were employed as early as 1884, although the school did not open until 1892. It is equally significant that, when the drive for reform in medicine culminated in the Flexner Report [1910], the Johns Hopkins Model was used as an example of what medical education should be [see Schlechty, 1984].)

3. A competent and distinguished group of teacher educators and researchers should be employed to staff the academy. This staff should be provided time to plan as well as complement new programs. In this regard, care should be taken not to limit the search for a staff to universities and traditional researcher institutions. Teacher educators (often staff developers) and researchers presently employed in public schools should also be recruited.

4. Existing institutions of higher education and existing teacher education programs should be invited and encouraged to participate in the invention of the academy. However, it is unlikely that those entities that now control teacher education will initiate the kinds of radical departures suggested by the academy. Early support for this change will probably come from outside the prevailing power structure (that is, outside of the governor's office, private foundations, and legislatures).

In conclusion, it is time for those inside the teacher education institution to accept the possibility that the problems they confront and the criticisms they receive are due more to outdated institutional forms than to their own lack of competence, quality of the knowledge they possess, or quality of the students they teach.

References

Biles, B. L., Billups, L. H., and Veitch, S. C. "Bridging the Gap: The AFT Educational Research and Dissemination Program." Paper presented at the annual meeting of the American Educational Research Association, Montreal, April 1983.

Clark, D. L., and Marker, B. "The Institutionalization of Teacher Education." In K. Ryan (Ed.), *Teacher Education.* (Seventy-fourth Yearbook of the National Society for the Study of Education, part 2, pp. 53-86.) Chicago: University of Chicago Press, 1975.

Dreeben, R. *The Nature of Teaching: Schools and the Work of Teachers.* Glenview, Ill.: Scott Foresman, 1970.

Drucker, P. F. *Management: Tasks, Responsibilities, Practices.* New York: Harper & Row, 1973.

Flexner, A. *Medical Education in the United States and Canada, Bulletin No. 4.* New York: Carnegie Foundation for the Advancement of Teaching, 1910.

Hovda, R. A., and Kyle, D. W. "Implementing Action Research in a Graduate Teacher Education Program." Paper presented at the annual meeting of the American Educational Research Association, Montreal, April 1983.

Howsam, R. B., Corrigan, D. C., Denmark, G. W., and Nash, R. J. *Educating a Profession: Report of the Bicentennial Commission on Education for the Profession of Teaching.* Washington, D.C.: American Association of Colleges for Teacher Education, 1975.

Lortie, D. C. *Schoolteacher: A Sociological Study.* Chicago: University of Chicago Press, 1975.

Nixon, J. A. *A Teachers' Guide to Action Research.* London: Grant McIntyre, 1981.

Schlechty, P. C. "Restructuring the Teaching Occupation: A Proposal." Paper commissioned by the American Educational Research Association, 1984.

Tikunoff, W. J., and Mergendoller, J. R. "Inquiry as a Means of Professional Growth: The Teacher as Researcher." In G. A. Griffin (Ed.), *Staff Development.* (Eighty-second Yearbook of the National Society for the Study of Education, part 2) Chicago: University of Chicago Press, 1983.
Waller, W. *The Sociology of Teaching.* New York: Wiley, 1932.
Whitford, B. L. "Some Structural Constraints Affecting Action Research." *The High School Journal,* 1984, *68* (1), 18-24.

Phillip C. Schlechty is executive director, Gheens Professional Development Center, Jefferson County Public Schools, and professor of educational administration, University of Louisville.

Betty Lou Whitford is research fellow at the Gheens Professional Development Center and assistant professor of secondary education at the University of Louisville.

The time is here for renewed support of existing laboratory schools and for the development of new ones.

A Bold "Old" Step: Return to Laboratory Schools

Ernest K. Dishner, Paula R. Boothby

"The last quarter of the twentieth century may well be distinguished by the emergence of the laboratory school as a productive center for educational inquiry, exerting powerful influence upon and shaping public education of the twenty-first century" (Hunter, 1970, p. 14).

Thus begins Madeline Hunter's *Phi Delta Kappan* article of 1970 entitled "Expanding Roles of Laboratory Schools." As we rapidly approach the twenty-first century, we wonder if the current small corps of laboratory schools will be able to fulfill Hunter's earlier prophecy.

In a 1973 article entitled "Teacher Education for the 1980s," Theodore R. Sizer suggests the need for improvements in teacher education on two fronts: First, he recommends that the quality of scholarly preparation and of the professional training of teachers be upgraded "through 'clinical' apprenticeship(s) in well-supervised, imaginative teacher complexes or centers" (p. 50). Second, he challenges teacher educators and schools of education to become more actively involved in "systematic and sustained inquiry" of the teaching process. Sizer concludes his thoughts about the importance of educational inquiry by stating: "Since no academic institution save the school of education now exists to champion such work, it is up to the teacher education fraternity to see that it happens" (p. 51).

The campus-based school provides the most appropriate site for well-structured clinical experiences for preservice teacher education students, and systematic and sustained study of teaching and learning (that is, for educational inquiry).

This chapter presents a brief summary of the development and decline of the laboratory school movement in this country; describes the functions of laboratory schools, first as laboratories for the education of future teachers and secondly as centers for research and experimentation; provides a description of one successful laboratory school; and offers some concluding thoughts.

The Development of Laboratory Schools

The laboratory school movement was initiated in this country in the early to middle nineteenth century. During the last half of that century, most teachers were trained in regular schools, which in turn operated laboratory schools that provided prospective teachers with a controlled environment in which to observe master teachers, to begin to teach, and to develop pedagogical skills. In 1890 the Teachers College, Columbia University, was established by Nicholas Murray Butler to "integrate more rigorous academic study and teacher training" (McPherson and McGee, 1982) into the study of education. Six years later, John Dewey founded the Laboratory School at the University of Chicago. Some historians credit Dewey with the establishment of the second major purpose for laboratory schools, namely, that they be centers for research and experimentation (McPherson and McGee, 1982).

Through the first half of the twentieth century, laboratory schools continued to serve first and foremost as campus-based sites for observations and for student teaching experiences (Hutton, 1965). Even into the 1960s, the primary functions of laboratory schools were observation and student teaching (Kelly, 1965). However, by the end of the 1960s, Howd and Browne (1970) reported a shift in the perceived importance of the student teaching function by laboratory school directors. More specifically, the perceived importance of student teaching as a laboratory school function dropped significantly. Even with this apparent shift of emphasis, the reduction in the number of laboratory schools continued through the 1960s and into the 1970s.

No single reason can be cited for the steady decrease in the number of laboratory schools during the post-World War II era. Rather, a variety of factors can be listed, including (1) the financial burden of operating laboratory schools; (2) the perception that the children taught in laboratory schools were not representative of the population teachers must teach; (3) the rapid development of state teachers' colleges into state colleges, and, eventually, to multi-purpose state universities; (4) the multiple staff roles and the attempt to serve too many functions; (5) the overuse of part-time, temporary faculty in the laboratory schools and the resulting loss of program continuity; (6) the development of the Teacher Corps model; (7) the increased emphasis on field experiences in the public school setting; (8) the competition with public schools for state support and for external grant dollars; and (9) the lack of systematic involvement by the faculty of schools and colleges of education in laboratory school activities.

Role of Laboratory Schools in Teacher Preparation

While the number of laboratory schools has declined, the professional literature continues to emphasize the need for laboratory and field experience.

Friedman and others (1980) suggest a hierarchy of laboratory and field experience activities as an integral part of an undergraduate teacher education program. The first experience in their hierarchy is the visitation, which is followed by observations, analyzing and critiquing, demonstrations, simulation, materials preparation, implementation of skills, and, finally, student teaching.

Cruickshank (1984) offers a similar, but less specific, listing of the types of experiences that should be required of preservice teachers. These field- or school-based experiences include *observations,* part-time *participation,* part-time *apprenticeships,* and full-time *practicum,* or student teaching. During the observation stage, the preservice teacher does not engage in real teaching, but instead systematically observes the process. Part-time participation involves real teaching in a structured setting, usually focusing on selected teaching skills that relate to teaching theory classes. Part-time apprenticeships provide preservice teachers with the opportunity to learn through practical experiences that are guided by skilled teachers. Finally, full-time practicums or student teaching involve an extended period of work in a classroom setting and significant responsibility for teaching larger units.

In the context of Friedman and others' (1980) hierarchy of laboratory or field experiences, the initial step—visitation—should take place in the broader off-campus community. This seems only reasonable, since the visitations should provide opportunities to view a variety of schools and programs. If possible, several visits to both public and private school settings should be arranged. Purposeful observations, however, should take place within the laboratory school setting in conjunction with professional education courses such as human growth and development and educational psychology or learning theory classes. Analyzing and critiquing teaching strategies, learning classroom management techniques, and using instructional materials should also take place in the laboratory school.

Demonstrations, or model lessons, might best be presented to preservice teachers via videotape in appropriate methods courses. In this way the course instructor systematically guides undergraduate students' understanding of the lesson. Laboratory faculty should play an important role in the development of these videotaped demonstration lessons. Simulation activities are best accomplished through role playing and microteaching situations in appropriate methods courses.

At the next level of the hierarchy, students prepare lessons in specific context areas for specific groups of youngsters. These mini-teaching activities should involve individuals or small groups of pupils, first in the laboratory school then in the public school setting. Finally, the student teaching semester should be scheduled in public or private school classrooms.

Teacher education programs that provide these systematic opportunities for the study of the teaching/learning process produce more than mere classroom technicians. Rather, they produce true students of education. As noted above, the role of laboratory schools in teacher education should be related almost exclusively to field experience activities that precede student teaching. In laboratory schools where large numbers of student teachers are placed, those preservice teachers involved in pre-student teaching field experiences often find that they are observing student rather than master teachers. This precludes the use of laboratory schools as the actual student teaching assignment. Furthermore, the culminating field experience just prior to certification—the student teaching experience—should take place at the school level for which certification will be granted.

Some argue (McPherson and McGee, 1982) that overemphasis on the teacher preparation function has diverted laboratory schools from their more important role, namely, innovation and experimentation. Focusing on specific aspects of the pre-student teaching field experience program will result in more time for research and experimentation.

Role of Laboratory School in Research and Experimentation

Hunter (1970), Sizer (1973), and Goodlad (1984), among others, have argued for the need for innovation and the importance of systematic educational inquiry. A laboratory school offers an almost ideal setting for research and experimentation. Unfortunately, much of the educational research conducted in laboratory schools (and, for that matter, in departments, schools, and colleges of education) is the result of the research interests of individuals. Furthermore, most educational research has been of a short-term nature and rarely relates to a larger research framework.

Collaborative research efforts that are well structured and systematically developed over a significant period of time can result in better understanding of the teaching/learning process. These have the potential for positively affecting public and private school practice. Laboratory schools offer the opportunity for collaboration and long-term research projects. McPherson and McGee (1982) cite the work done at the University of Hawaii since the mid-1960s as an example. Collaborative efforts there between laboratory school faculty and the University's curriculum research and development group have produced significant changes in the focus of the school.

A Successful Example

Although there are numerous outstanding laboratory schools throughout the country, the Malcolm Price Laboratory School provides an excellent and successful example. In May 1983 Malcolm Price Laboratory School observed its one-hundredth anniversary on the campus of the University of Northern Iowa. From its beginning in 1883, the Malcolm Price Laboratory School has served as a model school for students and faculty. The work of the faculty and staff of the Lab School has contributed significantly to the preparation of professional educators at the University of Northern Iowa and to the curriculum and instruction used by teachers and schools in the state of Iowa and the nation.

Ross Nielsen (1985), the long-time director of the Malcolm Price Laboratory School, has described the three basic functions of campus-based schools as (1) a laboratory for the preparation of educational personnel, (2) a laboratory for educational research, development, and innovation, and (3) a source of professional services to the faculty and students of the University and the teachers and schools of the state (1985).

Laboratory Schools for Preparation of Educational Personnel. All undergraduate teacher education students complete one or more pre-student teaching field experiences at the School, where they make structured observations or watch demonstrations. Even before these students arrive at the School, many have already viewed the students and teachers in one or more of their college classes on videotape. At the Lab School, all preservice teachers must complete a series of activities that are assigned by their instructors in courses on learning theory. These specific activities have been developed cooperatively by faculty from both the educational psychology department and the Lab School.

Laboratory for Educational Research, Development, and Innovation. Lab School faculty members are involved in a variety of collaborative research projects with other members of the College of Education and with faculty colleagues in other academic departments on campus. In addition, faculty develop and test a variety of materials in all curricular areas. Finally, research and grant proposals developed by the Lab School faculty help to support innovation in such diverse areas as metric education, computer technology, instructional strategies, and learning styles. Among other projects over the past decade, Lab School faculty members have developed curricular materials on the teaching of problem-solving skills in intermediate level mathematics and have coordinated a massive microcomputer project for middle and secondary school mathematics. The problem-solving materials, developed under Project IMPACT, are being used in all fifty states, and the Microcomputer Curriculum Project materials are being used by over 2 million students nationwide. These external projects, along with significant university support, have enabled the faculty of the Malcolm Price Laboratory School to make major contributions to innovation in the state's and nation's schools (Nielsen, 1985).

Source of Professional Service. The Malcolm Price Laboratory School has a long history of service to teachers and schools in the state of Iowa. The faculty has assumed an important leadership role in the delivery of significant professional conferences and workshops and is actively involved in conducting inservice programs, serving on school evaluation teams, providing consultative services, and delivering extension classes and workshops. A wide range of professional publications are available through its own publications, and faculty members are actively involved in the development of numerous commercially published textbooks, curriculum guides, tests, classroom resource and instructional materials, and microcomputer programs.

Some Final Thoughts

In *A Place Called School,* John Goodlad (1984) notes the significant contributions made by laboratory schools in the first half of this century but acknowledges that there is "little prospect of reincarnating the laboratory school movement of the past" (p. 300); however, Goodlad goes on to advocate the creation in each state of "a network of district-based schools specifically charged with the responsibility of developing exemplary practices extending beyond mere refinement of the conventional" (p. 300). These "key" schools "should be linked to universities and to each other in a communicating, collaborative network. There are simply not the resources in universities for serving many schools on an individual basis. But one university might well provide to a network of a dozen or more key schools a comprehensive evaluation program and potentially powerful ideas emerging from research and inquiry" (p. 301). It seems appropriate that current laboratory schools could become a natural part of "key" school networks. Not only would such networks profit from university involvement but also the university faculty would gain equally from such a collaborative effort.

The National Commission for Excellence in Teacher Education (1985) offers an important recommendation when it states that "states should encourage and assist the development and evaluation of experimental teacher education programs." The Commission provided a more detailed explanation of this recommendation.

> In considering experimental programs, we urge that states provide resources and support to colleges and universities that want to design, test, and evaluate new approaches in teacher education. Colleges and universities should be encouraged to consider major structural changes, not just course modification; and states should be willing to adjust existing regulations, with appropriate monitoring, to test the new models [p. 16].

The development of new and better laboratory schools and the restructuring of those that currently lack clear focus certainly fall within that recommendation.

Another recommendation by the National Commission for Excellence in Teacher Education (1985) is that a National Academy for Teacher Education be established. The proposed academy would serve symbolically, to recognize the importance of teacher education; and functionally, to provide a substantial corps of teacher educators with postgraduate experiences through an organized traineeship program. The Commission's recommendation is laudable, but the academy concept might be more effective at a regional or even state level. And what better place to establish such an academy than at centrally located state institutions of higher education with fully functioning laboratory schools!

The State of Virginia is investing almost $3.5 million of additional state funds during 1983 to 1986 in a single high school that has been designated as the Governor's Center for Educational Innovation and Technology (Chion-Kenney, 1985). Varina High School in Henrico County near Richmond has been selected to serve as that state's exemplary high school partly because its student population is representative of the state's as a whole. Varina's teachers have been charged with the responsibility "to design a career-ladder plan, to develop a curriculum model, to practice and demonstrate effective instructional strategies using the latest research, and to determine how technology could best be used to enhance learning" (p. 14). Chion-Kenney notes that "the Varina experiment represents the revival of a well-regarded, if now uncommon, educational institution: the laboratory school" (p. 15).

The Varina experiment creates a laboratory school that is not affiliated with a university. Its creation has helped officials in Virginia recognize the need for experimentation in curriculum and instruction. If they could formally link Varina High School to a university, these officials could provide future teachers with the opportunity to be intimately involved in educational inquiry.

Perhaps the time is here for renewed support of those laboratory schools that continue to exist and for the development of additional laboratory schools at selected universities in states and regions not now served by one or more campus-based schools. If one can learn from past failures, perhaps much stronger laboratories might be developed for the purpose of educational research and experimentation. As Dewey (1966) commented:

> Only the scientific aim, the conduct of a laboratory comparable to other scientific laboratories, can furnish a reason for the maintenance by a university of an elementary school. Such a school is a laboratory of applied psychology. That is, it has a place for the study of mind as manifested in the child, and for the search after materials and agencies that seem most likely to fulfill and further the conditions of normal growth.
>
> It is not a normal school or a department for the training of teachers. It is not a model school. It is not intended to demonstrate any one special idea or doctrine. Its task is the problem of viewing the education of the child in the light of the principles of mental activity and processes of growth made known by modern psychology. The problem by its nature is an infinite one [pp. 96–97].

According to Hunter (1970), if laboratory schools cease to exist, two major unsolved problems in education remain.

> One is the ever-widening gap between knowledge generated by educational research and practice in the classroom. The other problem is the critical need for an experimental laboratory to refine or field test theory in an environment uncontaminated by the very necessary restrictions imposed on public schools [p. 14].

Laboratory schools should serve an extremely important function in the preparation of future teachers, that is, of lifetime students of education. What better way to develop creative, knowledgeable teachers than to provide a stimulating environment that emphasizes the systematic study of teaching and learning—educational inquiry that involves both teacher educators and future teachers!

References

Chion-Kenney, L. "The Varina Mission: Testing Reform for Others." *Education Week*, 1985, *4* (27), 1, 14–15.

Cruickshank, D. R. *Models for the Preparation of America's Teachers*. Bloomington, Ind.: Phi Delta Kappan Educational Foundation, 1984.

Dewey, J. *The Child and the Curriculum: The School and Society*. Chicago: Phoenix Books, University of Chicago, 1966.

Friedman, M. I., Brinler, P. S., and Hayes, P. B. D. *Improving Teacher Education: Resources and Recommendations*. New York: Longman, 1980.

Goodlad, J. I. *A Place Called School: Prospects for the Future*. New York: McGraw-Hill, 1984.

Howd, M. C., and Browne, K. A. (Eds.). *National Survey of Campus Laboratory Schools*. Washington, D.C.: The American Association of Colleges for Teacher Education, 1970.

Hunter, M. "Expanding Roles of Laboratory Schools." *Phi Delta Kappan*, 1970, 52 (1), 14-19.

Hutton, H. "Historical Background of the Campus School in America." In P. W. Bixby and H. E. Mitzel (Eds.), *Campus School to a Research Dissemination Center*. University Park: Pennsylvania State University Press, 1965.

Kelly, E. H. *College-Controlled Laboratory Schools in the United States, 1964*. Washington, D.C.: The American Association of Colleges for Teacher Education, 1965.

McPherson, R. B., and McGee, G. W. "Laboratory Schools." In *Encyclopedia of Educational Research*. New York: Macmillan, 1982.

National Commission for Excellence in Teacher Education. *A Call for Change in Teacher Education*. Washington, D.C.: The American Association of Colleges for Teacher Education, 1985.

Nielsen, R. "Malcolm Price Laboratory School: A Century of Service." In T. R. Berg (Ed.), *Schools*. Cedar Falls: College of Education, University of Northern Iowa, 1985.

Sizer, T. R. "Teacher Education for the 1980s." In D. J. McCarty (Ed.), *New Perspectives on Teacher Education*. San Francisco: Jossey-Bass, 1973.

Ernest K. Dishner is dean of the School of Education, Southwest Texas State University, and previously served as associate dean of the College of Education, University of Northern Iowa.

Paula R. Boothby, chair of the education department, Texas Lutheran College, is a former faculty member at the Malcolm Price Laboratory School at the University of Northern Iowa.

Prospective teachers require a carefully planned curriculum that integrates realistic practice in all the activities of teaching with theory and research in pedagogy.

Integrating the Clinical Approach into Pedagogy Courses

Norma Nutter

The "clinical" approach to teacher education means having prospective teachers systematically observe, simulate, and actually perform the activities of teachers in a controlled environment, under close supervision, and with feedback on their performance and opportunity to relearn, *in conjunction with* their studies of theory and research in pedagogy and foundational disciplines. The concept is broad and not new (Flowers and others, 1948). It subsumes early field experiences, student teaching or internship, and a variety of other activities commonly found in teacher education programs. The emphasis in clinical education, however, is on designing and implementing a systematic, carefully articulated relationship between the body of professional knowledge and the prospective practitioner's ability to function effectively.

Instruction for future teachers that is solely or predominantly based in the traditional college classroom is divorced from the reality of school rooms and is necessarily predominantly theoretical, admonitory, or anecdotal. There is nothing wrong with theory per se; in fact, all teaching ought to be based on some theory of what one is doing and why. Admonition—telling future teachers what their obligations will be and what they should not do—is also necessary; and anecdote—sharing one's personal experience with students—is illustrative. However, theory, admonition, and anecdote alone cannot convey how particular precepts are to be translated into practice.

On the other hand, entirely field-based instruction, which a few people have advocated, is also deficient. This apprenticeship model assumes that teaching is a clearly defined and delimited technical craft learnable by imitating a practitioner. Teaching, however, is not merely a technical craft. In fact, one of the most pervasive and persistent characteristics of teaching is its *variability*. Groups of pupils and individual pupils differ greatly from each other; as children develop they are different from their earlier selves. The social contexts of schooling vary; and within the classroom, the events teachers must respond to and the variables they must control are relatively unpredictable. To ask prospective teachers to imitate only one model or a few models of teaching produces teachers who are very limited in their repertoire of behaviors.

To be effective, teacher education must combine theory and practice, admonition and example, and ideas and realistic experience in an integrated, carefully planned curriculum. The main goal of the clinical approach is to help prospective teachers bridge the gap between the pedagogical knowledge base (be it theory, research, logic, or conventional wisdom) and practice.

Guiding Principles

The clinical approach, as envisioned here, is based on three guiding principles.

1. *There must be a carefully graduated sequence of clinical activities throughout the preparation program.* Activities progress from easy to difficult, from simple to complex, with corresponding decreases in degree of control, artificiality of setting, and intensity of guidance provided and a corresponding increase in the depth of the prospective teacher's involvement and degree of responsibility.

In the early stage of the program, clinically based teacher education must concentrate on helping the college student begin to view schooling from the other side of the desk. As Lortie (1975, pp. 62-65) noted, everyone who has been through K-12 schooling thinks he knows how it should be done and has some very firm—and often mistaken or inadequate—ideas about what teaching involves. Beginning education students must learn to study children, teachers, teaching, and schools. They must go into the schools and observe real manifestations of the facts and concepts they have learned in the college classroom. And they must begin to practice the simpler forms of managing, instructing, and interacting with children.

In the middle stage, teacher education students should continue their study of teaching and begin to practice isolated skills in small steps, with ample opportunity for continued practice to a high level of mastery. In this stage the prospective teacher should learn that there are specific, discrete skills in teaching, what those skills are and their names, why some skilled behaviors are regarded as more appropriate than others, and how to perform them.

In the final stage, the prospective teacher should learn to integrate the specific concepts and skills of teaching and gradually assume the full teaching role. Traditionally, it has been student teaching's intention to fill this purpose; however, the experiences of many beginning teachers indicate that the traditional student teaching experience is probably too short to provide an adequate induction into the profession (Johnston and Ryan, 1983). The growing interest in internship and induction programs may eventually provide the time necessary to fully implement the clinical approach.

2. *The prospective teacher must be closely supervised in clinical activities and must receive feedback that is intense, specific, technical, and as often as possible, directly related to theory and research.* In general, students of teaching need more specific criticism of their performance than they typically have received, and that criticism should be expressed in a commonly held technical language derived from specific theories of teaching, learning, motivation, classroom management, and so on (Griffin, 1983).

Clearly, such intense supervision cannot be provided in the traditional college format of lecture, readings, and paper and pencil tests. Given the nature of the clinical approach, a more appropriate model would permit a *coaching* relationship, such as is found in the performing arts, sports, and clinical medicine. Both campus-based and field-based components of teacher education require a close, intense relationship between a skilled teacher educator and a few students. Some aspects of a clinically based program can be conveyed in conventional classes to larger groups of students. However, the main business of learning to teach requires a skilled teacher educator who can and who is permitted by the situation to *coach*— to demonstrate, design practice activities, observe students, critique and reteach, observe again, and so forth until each capable student masters the skills.

3. *The clinical approach must be integrated with the campus-based curriculum and must underlie and support the entire preparation program.* The preparation program thus forms a coherent whole balanced between the future practitioner's desire and need for practical assistance and the profession's need for practice informed by theory, research, and background knowledge.

The clinical approach is based in *realism*, that is, in relating college classroom teaching to school teaching through the actual objects and activities of school teaching. The objects and activities are not presented to the prospective teacher for unconscious absorption, but for conscious study, for imitation, and for creative construction of new objects and activities.

Examples of the Clinical Approach

Clinical activities occur in a variety of settings. Some occur in schools and in other agencies or organizations that serve children. These early field experiences are increasingly more common in teacher education programs. The clinical approach emphasizes a structured approach to the design and conscious, systematic use of these experiences in instructing prospective teachers. Clinical activities also occur in clinics and clinic-like settings, in campus classrooms, in media centers, and so on. Some activities are even performed outside the instructional program, as homework that will be critiqued later. Whatever teachers do can be observed, simulated, or actually performed by prospective teachers in whatever setting works best.

The most common type of clinical activity, particularly for the beginning students, is *observation,* simply watching teachers and children. Beyond acclimation to the classroom, however, unstructured observation contributes nothing to the prospective teacher's growth. As Friedman and others (1980) note, mere exposure to the classroom reduces "culture shock," but "for prospective teachers to benefit measurably from fieldwork, however, it is necessary to structure and process their observations and participation" (p. 10). In the clinical approach, observations must be structured, related to specific observational tasks, and associated with specific theories and concepts. And, most important, students must be debriefed about what they have observed and the relationship to what they are learning. A number of instruments exist for teaching preservice teachers to analyze what they see in classrooms (Ishler, 1981), and a multitude of guided observational activities are feasible (Mills, 1980). Examples of structured observational activities would include measuring how much time a discipline problem pupil spends engaged in learning activities versus unengaged time, noting how a teacher effects transitions between activities and evaluating the techniques for efficiency, or noting differences in groupings and activities on the playground by sex. Theoretical considerations related to these sample activities would include the relationship between time-on-task and learning; principles for effective communication, particularly of directions; and sex differences in social organization and play.

A second type of school-based clinical activity is assisting teachers in instructional management tasks (grading papers, housekeeping, collecting materials, preparing and using instructional materials and audiovisual aids, and planning) and in instructional tasks (supervising pupils; serving as a resource for pupils; tutoring; conducting small-group, large-group, and whole-group activities; and team teaching).

A third type of clinical activity is campus based, with a variety of possible activities:

1. *Simulations of preparation processes.* These activities take prospective teachers through the complex planning tasks of good teaching—selecting and preparing materials, designing units and lessons and all associated tasks, constructing tests, and so on—using either student-selected or instructor-assigned topics. In a coherent, well-designed clinical program, these simulated activities are accompanied by expectations that students provide specific rationales for their decisions, and the concrete products often are adapted later for use with pupils. Zuckerman (1979), for example, describes a simulation approach to a variety of administrative and planning tasks.

2. *Controlled practice.* Controlled practice activities include, first, clinical tutoring of pupils needing additional support in some area such as reading, mathematics, or study skills. Tutoring may focus on the prospective teacher's intended teaching specialty; however, it is useful for developing generic teaching skills as well. For example, any prospective teacher should be able to take a pupil's homework assignments and help the child organize his study time, learn material, practice skills, and prepare for tests. Similarly, any prospective teacher should be able to take a classroom teacher's or specialist's prescription for routine remedial work and, with guidance, implement it (Bates and Hutchinson, 1984).

Controlled practice also includes micro-teaching and peer teaching techniques, which have considerable support for their efficacy in research (Borg and others, 1970). Typically, the student prepares structured mini-lessons using specified strategies, methods, topics, and/or materials and presents them to small groups of either peers or pupils. For example, students might be required to prepare a lesson and intersperse brief periods of lecture with questions to check comprehension as well as higher order questions to promote thought. Usually, the mini-lessons are video- or audiotaped, then critiqued by student and instructor. This is followed, ideally, by the opportunity to reteach and to improve specific points. Micro-teaching helps prepare the prospective teacher for full-length demonstration teaching toward the end of the preparation program.

3. *Case studies.* Case studies are selected, structured representations of reality presented for analysis and study. They include examples of classroom events and situations in a variety of media (video- or audiotape, printed transcripts) and can be commercial or homemade. These materials may present examples of appropriate or inappropriate teaching behaviors, sequences of classroom activity for analysis and discussion, and various decision-making and problem solving activities. Emerging computer technology should expand the capacity of teacher educators to construct simulations and case studies for their students (Bush and Cobb, 1983–1984).

Case studies, while several steps removed from actual teaching, provide the student of teaching with a controlled setting that permits thoughtful analysis and discussion and thorough instruction on key points. Compared to field experience, case studies guarantee that crucial events will occur and be noticed by the student and provide a permanent record that can be replayed or reread for close study (Orlosky, 1974).

The activities listed above are not revolutionary in concept or approach. Most teacher education programs feature some or all of them. The difference is that, in the clinical approach, these activities must be selected, organized, and implemented to form a coherent whole. Inglis and others (1973) describe several competency-based instructional units that very clearly illustrate the clinical approach.

In the language arts example, the prospective teachers receive instruction in a particular diagnostic instrument; then they practice using the instrument with audio- or videotapes of pupils reading aloud. The instructor discusses the results of these practice diagnostic sessions and the various options a teacher might employ and then assigns readings related to theoretical and practical issues. Each teacher education student administers the instrument to a child, analyzes the results, prescribes appropriate materials and teaching strategies, and is evaluated accordingly. As a final step, the teacher education student would actually implement the instructional prescription in tutoring sessions.

In the mathematics unit, prospective teachers are given lectures on relating manipulatives to basic arithmetic concepts such as number and proportion. After an orientation to the mathematics laboratory, each student completes a series of self-instructional activities and designs a sample mathematics lesson using manipulatives, which he or she then teaches to the other class members.

In the science unit, prospective teachers use packaged materials to design an instructional unit for a fourth-, fifth-, or sixth-grade class. Topics might range from seed germination to combustion to social insects. Their instructor takes them through a detailed, step-by-step approach to planning and provides readings. As they prepare their unit, the prospective teachers must articulate rationales for their choices. Each teacher education student then teaches a lesson from his or her unit to an appropriate elementary class and is evaluated on the basis of a videotape of his or her teaching and a test covering the campus-based instruction.

The theoretical pedagogical content to be deliberately related to the activities described above might include, for example, learning theories, particularly how children best learn subject-related concepts and skills and how cognitive development proceeds; selecting, organizing, and sequencing content; motivational techniques, media techniques, including both design and production skills; classroom and instructional management skills, and evaluation of instruction.

Problems in Implementing the Clinical Approach

The clinical approach makes sense. Logic, professional experience, and research in how people learn all support it. Unfortunately, in actual practice, there are a number of obstacles to overcome.

First, the clinical approach requires that teacher education faculty must design the curriculum as a whole, which means that they must overcome the natural tendency, inherent in institutional patterns, to regard courses as individual property. They must collectively establish clinical activities as requisite parts of the program. Toward this end, faculty must also regard their students as a responsibility held in common. The focus on the student's ability to integrate theory and learning and the sequential nature of the experiences and expectations demand that marginal students not be sent on. Traditional collegiate patterns of scheduling and staffing interfere with the clinical approach. Hall and Jones (1976) describe how faculty and student roles change when the emphasis is on attainment of skills. Kindsvatter and Wilen (1982) describe a conceptual framework for clinical experience and describe sample instructional sequences.

Second, the clinical approach, done properly, costs far more than what institutions typically spend on teacher education programs. For example, early field experience, a major component of the clinical approach, also requires considerable administrative time, if it is managed well. If an institution has more than a handful of education students, field experience becomes a tremendous logistical task. Someone must (1) identify specific kinds of placements and match them to students and courses; (2) keep schools, teachers, and education students informed of dates, times, purposes, activities, and expectations; (3) maintain good public relations with multiple schools and school districts; (4) deal with major problems in student performance; (5) monitor students' attendance; (6) record evaluations of students' performance and document their participation; (7) arrange transportation; and (8) coordinate the design and regular evaluation of the field experience component. Not surprisingly, Feistritzer (1984) found that larger teacher education programs had the least amount of field-based clinical experience. Obviously, a teacher education program committed to field experience for its students must be able to make a large investment in supervisory, staff, and administrative time.

A good clinical program also needs some specific, and expensive, physical resources other than the traditional college classroom and the school classroom. Prospective teachers and teacher educators should have access to a wealth of curricular and instructional materials of all types, in all subject areas, and for all types of students—textbooks, workbooks, slides, films and filmstrips, audio recordings and tapes, tests and testing equipment, children's and young adults' literature and magazines, teaching implements, curriculum guides, packaged curricular materials and kits, gym equipment, art supplies, musical instruments, educational toys, and so on. The selection should be wide and current, well-catalogued, and maintained by specialized staff; and teacher educators should not need to scrounge for free materials or lend their own possessions, as many now do.

A clinically based program needs a comprehensive media center that includes all modern learning technology, including computers, and a good selection of equipment for preparing materials. Education students need access to and instruction in media—both how to simply use it and how to use it to enhance instruction. Further, the media center requires staff skilled in media instruction and financial support for maintenance, repair, and replacement of hard- and software.

A clinical program requires specialized facilities to provide intense, controlled, closely supervised experiences not feasible in field sites. Examples would include testing/tutoring rooms with one-way observation windows and facilities for videotaping; demonstration classrooms and laboratories, and facilities and equipment for such specialized functions as counseling; foreign language laboratory instruction; instruction in music, art, and physical education (regular and adapted), speech and hearing therapy, and other therapeutic purposes. At present, such facilities often are nonexistent, small and crowded, devoted primarily to units and functions of the institution other than teacher education, or constantly commandeered for other purposes.

Finally, clinical programs need healthy library resources for both students and faculty—books, periodicals, indexes and other reference works, document retrieval services, and so on—and competent librarians who are trained and interested in the field of education. One result of the clinical approach is that much of the acquisition of factual knowledge shifts from the traditional lecture to student self-directed study.

All of these physical resources are necessary, along with trained staff to organize and maintain collections and facilities and to keep the resources available at hours convenient for students and faculty. Furthermore, any initial investment for physical resources must be followed by continuing funding for maintenance, repair, and updating.

In addition to physical resources, the clinical approach makes heavy demands for personnel. In terms of both quality and number, the people directly responsible for educating future teachers are critical. Done properly, clinically based teacher education is labor intensive. Technology can certainly assist, but it cannot replace the close contact between a teacher of the art and science of teaching and the student of teaching. And the traditional formulas for funding and staffing teacher education are inadequate.

As an example of the special needs of clinical teacher education, proper supervision of field experience students is extremely time consuming. Often, a group of education students cannot be placed in one school;

each needs an individual placement in a separate classroom to maintain the appropriateness and realism of the experiences and to not overburden classroom teachers and schools. Supervisors then have a considerable demand on their time for travel, observation, and conferences with each student throughout the duration of the experience. As it is now, when we include field experience in our teacher education curricula, we have three options: skimp on supervision, overburden professors with supervisory duties, or farm out supervision to graduate students and other subprofessionals.

For another example, supervision of controlled practice activities is similarly time consuming for faculty and students. A good micro-teaching program requires time for instructing teacher education students in how they are to prepare their mini-lessons to specifications and in the theory and research supporting the strategies they are to demonstrate. For maximum effectiveness, this preparatory stage should include multiple demonstrations (live or recorded) of the desired behavior. Also, there must be time for every student to do his or her first micro-teaching session, perhaps group critique time, time for the student to review and analyze his or her performance several times, time for a focused critique from the instructor, and time to repeat the whole process for improvement. Conducting only one micro-teaching session for thirty students may take as much of an instructor's time as a regular three-credit-hour course.

Despite the obstacles to implementing the clinical approach, it works. We know that successful instruction in any complex skill requires that the student be provided with numerous demonstrations and clear instruction, which are followed by intensive practice and feedback. Beginners must begin with simple subskills and gradually assemble the subskills into the desired behavior through successive approximation. The clinical approach offers teacher education the only hope of reconciling the need to teach the pedagogical knowledge base with the absolute necessity that beginning teachers be practically competent.

References

Bates, G. W., and Hutchinson, C. M. P. "The Effects of Early Field Experience Tutoring in Reading on Secondary Majors' Attitudes, Expectations, and Teaching Effectiveness." Paper presented at the annual meeting of the American Educational Research Association, New Orleans, April 1984. [ERIC Document Reproduction Service Number ED 243 848.]

Borg, W. R., Kelley, M. L., Langer, P., and Gall, M. *The Mini-Course: A Micro-Teaching Approach to Teacher Education.* Beverly Hills, Calif.: Macmillan Educational Services, Far West Laboratory for Educational Research and Development, 1970.

Bush, W. S., and Cobb, P. "Using Computers in the Classroom: A Problem for Teacher Educators." *Action in Teacher Education,* 1983-1984, 5 (4), 9-14.

Feistritzer, E. C. *The Making of a Teacher: A Report on Teacher Education and Certification.* Washington, D.C.: National Center for Education Information, 1984.

Flowers, J. G., Patterson, A. D., Stratemeyer, F. B., and Lindsey, M. *School and Community Laboratory Experiences in Teacher Education.* Washington, D.C.: American Association of Colleges for Teacher Education, 1948.

Friedman, M. I., Brinler, P. S., and Hayes, P. B. D. *Improving Teacher Education: Resources and Recommendations.* New York: Longman, 1980.

Griffin, G. A. *Executive Summary of the Final Report of a Descriptive Study of Clinical Preservice Teacher Education.* (Report no. 9026.) Austin: The University of Texas at Austin Research and Development Center for Teacher Education, 1983.

Hall, G. E., and Jones, H. L. *Competency-Based Education: A Process for the Improvement of Education.* Englewood Cliffs, N. J.: Prentice-Hall, 1976.

Inglis, J. D., Gibney, T. C., Ahern, J. F., and Schaff, J. "CBTE and the Basic School Subjects." In G. E. Dickson and R. W. Saxe (Eds.), *Partners for Educational Reform and Renewal: Competency-Based Teacher Education, Individually Guided Education, and the Multiunit School.* Berkeley, Calif.: McCutchan, 1973.

Ishler, P. "Analyzing Teacher Behavior: Suggested Instruments for Preservice and Inservice Instruction." In R. MacNaughton and W. W. Wilen (Eds.), *Action in Teacher Education: A Responsible Program for the 1980s.* Kent, Ohio: Kent State University, 1981.

Johnston, J. M., and Ryan, K. "Research on the Beginning Teacher: Implications for Teacher Education." In K. R. Horney and W. E. Gardner (Eds.), *The Education of Teachers: A Look Ahead.* New York: Longman, 1983.

Kindsvatter, R., and Wilen, W. "A Clinical Experience Theory Applied to Clinical Practice." *Action in Teacher Education,* 1982, *4* (2), 17-26.

Lortie, D. C. *Schoolteacher: A Sociological Study.* Chicago, Ill.: University of Chicago Press, 1975.

Mills, J. R. "A Guide for Teaching Systematic Observation to Student Teachers." *Journal of Teacher Education,* 1980, *21* (6), 5-9.

Orlosky, D. E. "The Protocol Materials Program." *Journal of Teacher Education,* 1974, *25* (4), 291-297.

Zuckerman, R. A. "Simulation Helps Preservice Students Acquire Pragmatic Teaching Skills." *Journal of Teacher Education,* 1979, *30* (4), 14-16.

Norma Nutter is assistant dean of the College of Education at the University of Northern Colorado.

If the teaching profession, state education agencies, and national accrediting bodies rigorously apply standards now widely acknowledged as desirable for teacher education, the number of teaching programs will be very substantially reduced.

The Reduction in Teacher-Preparation Institutions: Rationale and Routes

Hendrik D. Gideonse

The central propositions of this chapter are three. What we know about teaching and learning means that we are capable of designing and delivering much more sophisticated and effective teacher preparation experiences. When the specific requirements of such programs are examined, however, it becomes clear that the instructional resources available for teacher preparation in America are too thinly distributed and improperly structured to carry out the kind of professional training that ought to exist. If and when such convictions are acted on, there will be a substantial decline in the number of teacher education programs and of institutions engaging in the preservice preparation of teachers. Such ideas must be included among the education profession's "dangerous thoughts."*

The current ferment over teacher education and its standards attests

---

*Evidence that this circumstance is so may be found in the reactions of teacher educators to a policy report distributed in 1981 to all schools, colleges, and departments of education in the country (Tucker and others, 1984). The report predicted that some number far smaller than the then-current number of institutions would be able to mount the kind of preparation programs on which the

to the centrality of this issue in the achievement of educational reform, such as: the testing of teachers (before and after entry into teaching); the development of alternate routes to certification (ranging from legitimate preparation models to the virtually complete bypass of responsible training); the growing recognition of real differences between preservice, induction, and inservice education of teachers; career ladders; recruitment of foreign nationals into American teaching settings; teacher evaluation; merit pay; the movement toward professional practices boards; and the increased attention to heightened standards for teacher education institutions by the National Council for the Accreditation of Teacher Education (NCATE) and by the collection of institutions that have styled themselves the Holmes Group (Currence, 1985a; Currence, 1985b). These disparate proposals testify to the dramatic change in the context now confronting institutions of higher education responsible for preservice teacher education. (For a complete summary of initiatives taken in the states, see American Association of Colleges for Teacher Education, 1985.) It would seem, therefore, an apposite time to confront directly the possibility that the next two to three decades should see a real and substantial reduction in the number of teacher education programs and institutions.

The Current Distribution and Two Possible Reasons for Reduction

Currently, some 1,241 institutions of higher education in America are approved by their respective states to offer some 7,233 different certification programs (Roth and Mastain, 1984). This large number *excludes* the different certifications awarded to subject matter specialties for secondary education certificates. National Center for Education Statistics (NCES) data show that the degree productivity of 1,191 institutions that actually awarded baccalaureate degrees in education in 1977 to 1978 ranges from a single graduate (twenty-five such institutions) to one university that graduated 1,035. More than a quarter of the institutions produced 25 education baccalaureates or fewer. More than half produced fewer than 50. These numbers, admittedly dated but drawn from the only detailed data currently available to the author, have declined still further. In fall 1980, the author requested a special printout from the National Center for Education Sta-

---

profession of teaching should be built. The response was swift. Outrage was communicated back to those who prepared the report (Tucker, 1984, p. 38), and Terrell Bell, U.S. Secretary of Education at the time, received an impassioned letter from individuals representing smaller departments of education suggesting funding be cut off for the policy inquiry unless the bias perceived to be present in the recommendations was addressed.

tistics that arrayed institutions in descending order of degree productivity in education in the 1977-78 academic year. Baccalaureate degrees were awarded by 1,191 institutions, master's by 676, and doctoral degrees by 164. A total of 1,243 different institutions awarded education degrees of one kind or another. One aspect of the data that does not tend to increase one's confidence in its accuracy is the discrepancy between the 1978 figure for education baccalaureate degrees awarded as reported in the *Statistical Abstract of the United States for 1984*—136.1 thousand (U.S. Bureau of the Census, 1983, p. 169)—and the total developed manually from the NCES printout for 1977-78—137.3 thousand.

The number of institutions preparing teachers seems to have remained about the same (1,243 granted education degrees of some kind in 1978 as compared to the 1,241 listed in the National Association of State Directors of Teacher Education and Certification materials for 1984), but the aggregate number of degrees awarded dropped nearly ten thousand a year from 136,000 in 1978 to 108,000 in 1981. While detailed data about all teacher education institutions in America are hard to obtain, what we do have permits us to say with a certainty that a very large number of institutions in America are approved for teacher preparation for an even larger number of certification purposes and, while certainly an important activity to them, the majority of institutions produces quite small numbers of teachers eligible for certification. Data compiled by NCATE embrace less than half the teacher education institutions in America. Data available from AACTE cover a somewhat larger but still barely 60 percent subsample. Data collected by Emily Feistritzer's National Center for Educational Information, while getting very substantial play in the media, are notoriously soft. Making national policy for a societal function as vital and as decentralized as teacher education is greatly complicated by the incompleteness and weakness of available data.

The reduction in the number of teacher education programs will occur because of the articulation and application of standards for teacher education that are substantially different and substantially higher than at present. The reduction will take place in two ways. Some institutions, looking at the standards, will see they cannot meet them and withdraw. Others, believing that they meet the standards, will present themselves for approval by state or national bodies and fail to receive it.

Teaching ought to be a profession. Training for that profession ought to take place as it does for other professions, in a higher education setting especially dedicated to that function. While clinical learning is crucial eventually to successful performance in teaching, its intellectual requirements and what is known about teaching and human learning are sufficiently deep, complex, and sophisticated to rule out apprenticeship training models as acceptable modes of entry.

Teacher Education Standards

The Role of Standards in Defining a Profession. Standards are necessary for professional status, but, of course, not sufficient. All professions place great emphasis on their special knowledge (and implicitly, therefore, on the importance of empirically grounded action). Professions, however, are defined as much by the values they serve as the knowledge they employ (Green, 1984). Standards, whether for performance or preparation for performance, embody the "ought" statements that provide essential definition of the profession in question.

Knowledge Base Standards. One powerful element in teacher education reform in recent years has been attention to the knowledge bases that underpin sound professional practice, and therefore, preparation for that practice. This theme has not been without its controversies, critics (for example, Tom, 1984 and Green, 1984), or detractors. In the main, however, teacher educators recognize that over the longer haul the profession of teaching and its subspecialty, teacher education, can ill afford to ignore the obligation to form clear judgments about what knowledge and related skills are of most worth to practitioners and to assure that entrants into the profession have a strong preparation in these areas. (Indeed, the draft NCATE standards adopted for comment in June 1985 and projected for approval in October 1985 include as one of the five major groupings of standards one titled "Knowledge Base for Professional Preparation" [National Council for the Accreditation of Teacher Education, 1985, pp. 16-19].) There is fairly wide agreement that the essential knowledge bases for professional performance in teaching include (see, for example, National Education Association, 1982, and American Association of Colleges for Teacher Education, 1983):

1. A liberal education, conceived, not just as a measured distribution of courses, but in terms of the achievement of a number of goals, for example: the capacity of expression, linguistically and artistically; acquisition of analytic and decision-making skills; cultural awareness of one's own and other's, including the sense of how one's own functions and how it has developed over time; modes of developing human knowledge; discourse and action in the values domain; and so on.

2. Mastery of the curriculum content in the areas for which the teacher is to be responsible.

3. Mastery of the intellectual foundations of the profession, including an awareness of its historical, sociological, philosophical, psychological, and anthropological roots.

4. Mastery of the full array of professional understandings and skills, including:
   - Human development and learning
   - Principles of effective practice

- Evaluation, inquiry, and research pertaining to education
- Educational goals and objectives
- Educational policy
- Cultural influences on learning
- Curriculum planning and design
- Planning, management, and delivery of instruction, including strategies for exceptionalities
- Design and use of evaluation and measurement methods
- Classroom and behavior management
- School law, including due process requirements
- Instructional technology
- Collaborative and consultative skills*.

Standards Respecting Connection to Practitioners. New standards also seek to establish more effective connections between teacher educators and the experience and knowledge of practitioners and the realities of the responsibilities with which practitioners are charged.

The impetus for the development of standards in this area arises from several influences. One of these has been the increasing insistence of teachers' organizations that they have a stronger role in the design and evaluation of teacher education programs. Another has been the recognition by teacher educators that the larger profession of education embraces teacher education but is not defined by it.

All educators are more aware of real differences that exist among schools and the various client populations served by schools. If certification is a license entitling a teacher to teach anywhere, much closer liaison with the actual and varied conditions of professional practice is needed. Also, in any profession prepared for in higher education, perennial tensions exist between the theoretical and the applied, between conceptual underpinnings and practical realities.

Resource Standards. The penury afflicting teacher preparation in America's colleges and universities has been well established (Peseau and Orr, 1980). That condition is both absolute and relative. Teacher education programs are the least well supported professional preparation programs in American higher education. More important, they are insufficiently supported to accomplish their own stated objectives.

Resources, of course, are of several different kinds. They include time, money, talent, environments, facilities and equipment. Resources are always relative to demand; a $5 million program with 120 faculty may be 50 percent underfunded, while a program budgeted at $200,000 with

---

*This listing of requisite knowledge in the professional domain was abstracted from the final Draft Standards of the National Council for the Accreditation of Teacher Education adopted for public comment at its June 7, 1985 meeting in St. Louis.

but 3 faculty might appear well off but actually be seriously undersupported on other than financial terms.

Resource standards, therefore, speak to such requirements as:
- Adequate facilities for clinical instruction
- Adequate faculty/student ratios to support supervision of clinical work
- Faculty instructional loads that guarantee opportunities for scholarly activity
- Adequate instructional materials and equipment
- Resources for faculty development and professional engagement
- Proximity and access to diverse clinical settings
- Sufficient faculty with appropriate advanced training to serve the intellectual and professional requirements of the program.

How Adherence to These Standards Will Reduce the Number of Teacher Education Programs

Five key factors should substantially diminish the number of institutions currently engaged in teacher education. (The word "should" is intended here not in its predictive sense alone, but in its normative, "ought" sense as well.) The institutions affected will be of many different kinds. The five factors are:

1. An insufficient range of professional teacher education faculty possessing advanced training in the specialties they are expected to contribute to the teacher education program.

2. The inability or unwillingness to offer a set of curricular opportunities for teacher education students designed and delivered so as to give promise of achieving the liberalizing aims of general education.

3. The absence of sufficient resources for teacher education faculty to be able to engage in the kind of reflective inquiry that ought to characterize a professional training program and environment.

4. Failure to maintain a teacher education program that itself is delivered according to the precepts of best practice it seeks to transmit.

5. Inability to support and provide access to clinical sites sufficient not merely to acquaint teaching candidates with the diversity they are likely to encounter but to equip them to work effectively with it.

Insufficient Arrays of Professionally Prepared Faculty. The great majority of teacher education programs in America, whether in small institutions or large, are staffed with a very small number of faculty.

This assertion is based, in part, on logical extrapolation from the figures cited earlier. The majority of teacher preparation programs graduate very few teachers. Other sources (for example, Peseau and Orr, 1980) show that teacher education programs in general are not staffed abundantly. In Ohio, state subsidy to teacher preparation programs is based on a formula that assumes a 20 to 1 student/faculty ratio. (In order to drop that ratio to 14 to 1, more consistent with the instructional obligations of a clinical preparation program, a special legislative appropriation for teacher education has had to be passed for each of the past ten years.) While the new NCATE standard calls for a ratio of 18 to 1 for the clinical portions of the program (NCATE, 1985, p. 30), even that figure is projected as a real challenge for many institutions.

Add one more element to the equation. That is the amount of a student's baccalaureate program devoted to just the professional portion of the teacher education program, that which is provided by the teacher education faculty themselves. Reasonable estimates would suggest slightly less than a year's work is currently required for most secondary certificates. Considerably more is required for elementary, special education, or K-12 certification (such as art, music, or physical education specializations). A very conservative average of the two, then, would indicate that one and one-third full-time equivalent (FTE) years of effort are reflected in each baccalaureate graduate. If 20 to 1 is taken as the ratio of students to faculty in initial certification on the average across the nation, the conclusion may be drawn that the overwhelming majority of teacher preparation programs are staffed with very small numbers of faculty, indeed. Using these calculations, a program graduating fifty teachers a year would probably have only a little over three full-time equivalent education faculty (50 graduates times 1.33 student FTEs divided by 20 = 3.25 faculty FTE).

This logical analysis was partially confirmed by data developed from college catalogues in Ohio. Forty-eight institutions are approved for teacher education in Ohio. After the twelve large state universities and the largest private university, it was possible to develop estimates of the number of education faculty in thirty-four of the remaining thirty-five (one catalogue did not list current faculty). These institutions broke into two groups, a cluster of seven averaging nearly sixteen faculty per institution and the remainder, which averaged just over four faculty per institution. Two offsetting considerations should be mentioned. Faculty associated with health and physical education were not counted because, in the catalogues examined, many of the athletic department coaches carry such titles. On the other side of the ledger, some institutions did not distinguish between full- and part-time faculty either by grouping or title. Such faculty were considered all full time for the purposes of this analysis, thus tending to inflate the averages. One final consideration is the existence in Ohio of a very specific 14 to 1 student/faculty ratio standard and a rigorous state evaluation process. The figures shown, therefore, may very well be richer than for similar institutions in other states.

Whether the average faculty size for small programs is one, three, or five makes little difference. That number, from the professional claim and stance adopted here, is simply too small to be able to provide the kind of academic and professional faculty, instruction, and curricular offerings that teaching candidates require (see parts three and four of the previous listing of knowledge bases focusing on the professional portion of the program). Sufficient expertise in those areas could not be developed, maintained, or delivered to students with five full-time faculty, let alone with a smaller number. Exact specification of the minimum number would be difficult, if not foolish, because of a host of indeterminate variables, including individual capacities, institutional character, and curricular design differences. The academic specialties, however, that directly bear on parts three and four of the professional portions of the program include at least eighteen distinct areas. Even allowing for some modest doubling up, it is difficult to see how a professional program could justify being staffed with fewer than twelve to fifteen faculty, simply on the basis of specializations. Even that number might be pushing it in light of the need for teacher education faculty to have time, in addition to their instructional duties, to also engage in reflective inquiry about their responsibilities.

Small institutions will *not* be the only ones at risk. Many large institutions currently operate one or more professional preparation programs for teaching on a basis that is little better than that which smaller institutions muster. In addition, rigorous application of the standards involved here should also jeopardize the future role of teacher education programs in larger institutions, which have chosen to staff them heavily with advanced graduate students.

Acting on the professional implications of extant knowledge bases for teaching and teacher education will necessarily lead to the eventual removal from teacher preparation of all those programs inadequately staffed for the responsibilities they have assumed.

Failure to Deliver a Liberalizing Education to Teaching Candidates. The obligation for teacher education programs to provide their graduates with a liberal education, if enforced, could have the effect of removing some, perhaps even many, large institutions from the ranks of teacher education. In truth, not many of America's institutions of higher education are currently meeting their responsibilities here. But the difficulties in doing so will clearly be greatest in large institutions. The narrow academic professional proclivities of the faculty and the absence of real incentives or rewards for undergraduate instruction aimed at the purposes of liberal education conspire to make such activities very low priority.

Defining, designing, and delivering curricula that achieve the liberalizing aims requisite for responsible professional practice in teaching is demanding, time-consuming intellectual work. It takes great commitment on the part of any institution. It takes a special environment within the faculty. It takes a differentiated reward structure and vigorous academic leadership. Paradoxically, especially in light of the implications of other aspects of the argument advanced in this chapter, small and medium-sized institutions are far more likely to be able to succeed at this than large, research-oriented ones (see Gideonse, 1984).

Lack of Commitment to Faculty Loads That Balance Teaching Duties with the Obligation to Engage in Inquiry. It is difficult to imagine how society could accept any kind of professional preparation program that exists in the absence of an environment of reflective inquiry. But how can this environment exist when such heavy demands are made on teacher education faculty to just perform in their teaching and advising roles? Teacher education is notorious for the instructional loads placed on its faculty, and therefore, for the lack of time for inquiry and scholarship.

The instructional demands on teacher educators are heavy for several reasons. Good programs have a heavy dose of clinical instruction that, even apart from travel time, is inherently labor and time instensive. The excessively crowded "life space" of teacher education in the baccalaureate program increases instructional pressure. The numerous legitimate requirements of the certification process place heavy monitoring and advising demands on individual faculty. Finally, the present "culture" of teacher education nationally seems to be, in the main, oriented more to human and service concerns than to inquiry and scholarship.

State and national accreditation standards have long registered expectations that faculty in teacher preparation programs should engage in scholarship. Rarely, if ever, however, have negative decisions been made on this point. If a truly professional preparation program is to be mounted and sustained, lip service will have to give way to forthright action. When it does, two different kinds of institutions will be affected.

The first kind will be those where the programs are staffed insufficiently in the first place. Instructional demands of students and of certification will *always* take precedence. Inquiry expectations for professional preparation programs only place additonal demands on the current plurality of already inadequately staffed programs.

Some research-oriented institutions may also be in difficulty on this score, to the extent that inquiry there is actually being done by faculty other than those in teacher preparation. Teacher educators themselves must be committed to and engaged in inquiry. It is not enough for their colleagues to be so engaged.

Failure to Model Best Practice. Teacher educators often espouse the rhetoric of modeling best practice. Up until now, however, that idea has been addressed, if at all, at the more atomistic level of individual faculty performance. The incentive structure for reappointment, promotion, tenure, and merit awards has been the shaping instrument, not the standards applied to unit review or approval.

Recognition that teacher education programs and institutions should be held accountable for clinical fidelity, for *delivering* their professional preparation according to the knowledge bases that exist (that is, according to the same precepts of best practice that teacher educators seek to pass on to their students), is for the first time embodied in national accreditation language (NCATE, 1985, p. 16). Presuming that the standards are enforced, the impact will fall universally on all the different types and sizes of institutions now preparing teachers.

It will probably prove difficult for many institutions to meet this standard. Reasons include the inability to allocate faculty time to the continuous faculty development needs thus created and to the needed programmatic monitoring and quality control mechanism. Cultural norms in higher education may also intervene. Individual faculty may resist the notion that their instruction should be a matter of collegial concern. The widespread belief that any Ph.D. automatically confers on the bearer the requisite skills of teaching may interfere. A main difficulty, however, will be a "cost-of-doing-professional-preparation" claim on scarce resources that some institutions will find difficult to meet. (For further explication of the concept of clinical fidelity, see H. D. Gideonse, "Do As I Do, Which Is the Same As I Say," forthcoming in the *Journal of Thought*.)

Inability to Support and Provide Access to Diverse Clinical Sites. Teacher preparation programs have two obligations concerning clinical instruction. The first is to provide adequate clinical supervision. The second is to provide access to the range of clinical sites that will assure that graduates are equipped to deal with the diverse clients they might eventually serve. These obligations fall particularly heavily on one class of institutions—those situated in rural areas.

The obligation to provide clinical supervision of practice is troublesome to rural institutions for two reasons. The first is finding sufficient sites. To be sure, finding adequate sites is often difficult in urban areas, too, especially if the teacher preparation programs are at all selective about where students are placed. In rural areas, however, the total number of sites is sharply limited. A second difficulty, however, then enters in the form of the consumption of expensive faculty resources in traveling back and forth to the students' placements. The most common resolution of this problem is through a reduction in the number of supervisory observations by teacher education faculty. Teaching is a highly complex activity, and three or four hour-long observations can hardly accomplish the evaluative/developmental objectives of clinical supervision. Teacher education then effectively becomes theoretical preparation followed by a kind of apprenticeship with cooperating teachers who may have little advanced preparation themselves and who, typically, have next to no formal preparation for the clinical responsibilities with which they are charged. Coping satisfactorily with these two problems in rural settings is likely to make teacher education programs quite expensive.

The other kind of problem faced by rural programs cannot be resolved by resource allocation. Teacher education programs that seek to fulfill the professional needs of teaching candidates to become skilled at working with culturally diverse student populations will have a difficult time in most rural settings. While some diversity does exist, nothing like what is found in virtually every urban and suburban setting exists in rural America. While no urban or suburban area in America is very far removed from rural areas, many rural areas are very distant from urban and suburban settings with their great ethnic and cultural diversity. Rigorous application of state and national standards on preparing teachers for culturally pluralistic America would jeoparadize the future of many rural teacher preparation programs.

Routes to Reform: Issues and Implications

The preceding material presents the rationale for the reduction of the number of teacher preparation programs and institutions based on rigorous application of standards now widely agreed to be desirable. Its argument is the logical extrapolation of professional definitions and commitments increasingly articulated by teacher and teacher education organizations and agencies.

If the standards described in this chapter are applied, teacher education programs will be substantially reduced in number. Substantially would have to be interpreted as meaning a reduction of anywhere from one-half to two-thirds of the institutions now approved for such purposes. (Examination of the 1977-1978 NCES data shows that the net effect on overall productivity of certificated teachers would be much less severe. If we look only at numbers of graduates as an indicator of faculty size, which in turn is a measure of the array of specializations available for teacher preparation, the last 50 percent of producers yields but 9 percent of the supply. The last two-thirds of the producers generated but 20 percent of the total baccalaureate productivity in 1978. The last institution in the high third, however, graduated but ninety-five.)

The rationale for reduction poses serious questions:

1. How could and should such wholesale changes in teacher education take place in a fashion that is fair, just, and humane? Honest, hardworking, committed people have devoted their lives and professional careers to a function that now faces wholesale change. Is that commitment simply to be coldly thrown away and ignored?

2. The position advanced here starts from the premise of the knowledge bases underpinning teaching and learning and logical derivations from that premise. What will happen when teacher education encounters the intersections between what it knows and the politics that surround and pervade it?

3. Is it relevant to talk in terms of a timeline for the forthcoming reduction, especially in light of the widely decentralized decisions that must be made?

4. What is the likelihood of all this in view of the market pressures created by the resurgent demand for teachers? In the face of the substantial

enrollment decline in teacher education, precipitated mainly by low salaries and accurate perceptions of the problematic conditions of professional practice in the nation's schools, how can teacher education overcome its own particular Gresham's Law?

There are no easy answers to these questions. A combination of two ideas, however, appears especially promising. First, our conception of teacher education should be divided into two distinct phases: baccalaureate and postbaccalaureate. The baccalaureate phase of teacher preparation should concentrate on liberal education, curricular content, and that preparatory work necessary to establishing the intellectual foundations for teaching as a profession. The postbaccalaureate phase should encompass a new and much more sophisticated two-year professional preparation sequence (Smith, 1980; Gideonse, 1983).

Dividing and sequencing responsibility for liberal education and content mastery from professional preparation would ensure that every institution now engaged in teacher education could expect to maintain a significant role therein, albeit it in newly differentiated and defined ways. Some four hundred institutions, however, would continue in professional preparation per se.

Small and medium-sized institutions are the most likely to be able to serve the ends of teacher education's liberal education underpinnings (Gideonse, 1984). Other institutions, those already familiar with the obligations of postbaccalaureate professional preparation, are more likely to be able to meet the full range of expectations of the professional portion of knowledge-based teacher education.

Second, to focus and concentrate existing teacher education resources in the country, the fifty states should undertake a coordinated, ten-year, subsidized relocation of teacher educators who wish to move from small programs to better staffed programs, those with greater promise of being able to meet more rigorous knowledge-based standards. This proposal should receive very careful consideration by chief state school officers, NCATE, and the Education Commission of the States.

Teacher education faculty in smaller programs have exhibited commitment to a professional mission, which has recently changed. That commitment ought not to be lost or downplayed. A ten-year program of subsidized relocation to larger programs and institutional settings would provide an effective and fair buy-out period (or, alternatively, provide for retraining) that could be planned for and absorbed by the host institution after that period of time.

Assuming an average three faculty per small program would suggest a placement need for 2,400 faculty. (If the number were five, that would mean a need for 4,000 subsidized positions.) Spread over the fifty states and recognizing the salary structures of smaller institutions, the total dollar commitment would probably not exceed $120 million a year for the larger number of positions. It would be a small price to pay for accomplishing the professional transformation of teacher preparation in the course of a single decade. (This estimate makes no provision for retirements; the actual cost might be substantially less, since many who might otherwise need to be covered would, on grounds of forthcoming retirement, elect not to be included.)

The rationale for public responsibility for subsidizing relocation stems directly from the public responsibility for the certification function. Public authorities have, for the last several decades, sanctioned and sustained the current number of teacher preparation programs and institutions. Twelve hundred institutions have been, in effect, *encouraged* by public authorities to remain in teacher education. Professional and public recognition of the quantum leap now possible should, therefore, be recognized by the public authorities that have long supported the present configuration.

One final comment on a real danger. Teacher education must confront its own Gresham's Law, the extent to which market demands for teachers have been met so frequently in the past by lowered standards. In teaching, demand has not led to greater economic incentives as trained personnel become more scarce and more valuable. Instead, education has resorted to so-called temporary certificates or has reduced standards. In light of that regrettable reality, the only responsible way to view this problem is as a test of the profession's will and moral fiber. Teacher educators and the organized profession must insist that quality programs meet standards such as those defined in this chapter. We must stand resolute against the use of temporary certificates, creation of bypass routes to certification, lowered standards, or equivocal application of otherwise high standards. When we do this, the most powerful influence on quality graduates will become the rigor and sophistication of the teacher education programs themselves. Those programs will then function as the surest and most legitimate screen that could be imagined. The consequences for role, conditions of professional practice, salary, and performance would be swift and tangible.

References

American Association of Colleges for Teacher Education (AACTE). *Educating a Profession: Profile of a Beginning Teacher.* Washington, D.C.: American Association of Colleges for Teacher Education, 1983.

American Association of Colleges for Teacher Education (AACTE). *Teacher Education Policy in the States: Fifty-State Survey of Legislative and Administrative Actions.* Washington, D.C.: American Association of Colleges for Teacher Education, May 1985.

Currence, C. "Deans Considering Tougher Standards in Teacher Training." *Education Week,* June 5, 1985a, pp. 1, 18.

Currence, C. "Major Universities Adopt Tougher Teacher-Training Requirements." *Education Week,* June 12, 1985b, p. 5.

Gideonse, H. D. *In Search of More Effective Service: Inquiry as a Guiding Image for Educational Reform in America.* Cincinnati, Ohio: University of Cincinnati, 1983.

Gideonse, H. D. "A Future for Liberal Arts Colleges in the Preparation of Teachers." In A. R. Tom (Ed.), *Teacher Education in Liberal Arts Settings: Achievements, Realities, and Challenges.* Washington, D.C.: American Association of Colleges for Teacher Education, 1984.

Green, T. "The Knowledge Base for Teaching and Teacher Education." Paper presented at the Fall Meeting, Association of Colleges and Schools of Education in State Universities and Land Grant Colleges, Las Vegas, Nevada, October 7, 1984.

National Council for the Accreditation of Teacher Education (NCATE). *NCATE Redesign.* April 1985.

National Education Association (NEA). *Excellence in Our Schools: Teacher Education—An Action Plan.* Washington, D.C.: National Education Association, 1982.

Peseau, B., and Orr, P. "The Outrageous Underfunding of Teacher Education." *Phi Delta Kappan,* 1980, pp. 100-102.

Roth, R. A., and Mastain, R. *The NASDTEC Manual.* Sacramento, Calif.: National Association of State Directors of Teacher Education and Certification, 1984.

Simon, H. A. *The Sciences of the Artificial.* Cambridge, Mass.: The M.I.T. Press, 1969.

Smith, B. O. *A Design for a School of Pedagogy.* Washington, D.C.: U.S. Government Printing Office, 1980.

Tom, A. R. *Teaching as a Moral Craft.* New York: Longman, 1984.

Tucker, S. B. "Responses to the Policy Inquiry on Increasing the Research Capacity of Schools of Education." In H. D. Gideonse and E. A. Joseph (Eds.), *Increasing Research Capacity of Schools of Education: A Policy Inquiry and Dialogue.* Cincinnati: Fleuron Press, 1984.

Tucker, S. B., and others. "Increasing the Research Capacity of Schools of Education: A Policy Inquiry, March 1981." In H. D. Gideonse and E. A. Joseph (Eds.), *Increasing Research Capacity of Schools of Education: A Policy Inquiry and Dialogue.* Cincinnati: Fleuron Press, 1984.

U.S. Bureau of the Census. *Statistical Abstract of the United States 1984.* Washington, D.C.: U.S. Government Printing Office, 1983.

Hendrik D. Gideonse is professor of education and policy science and dean of the College of Education, University of Cincinnati.

Liberal arts colleges have had a long and distinguished record of excellence in teacher preparation that has been made possible by their unique characteristics and mission.

Private Liberal Arts Colleges and Teacher Preparation

Norene F. Daly

What are the distinctive characteristics of teacher preparation programs in private liberal arts colleges and what continuing role will these colleges play in the education of our nation's teachers? The purpose of this chapter is to (1) explore the emergence of private liberal arts colleges as institutions where teacher education has become an important mission, (2) focus on the unique characteristics of governance within private liberal arts colleges and the effect on teacher preparation, (3) review the content of teacher preparation programs within these colleges and examine how they compare to programs in public colleges and universities, (4) review problems currently encountered by private liberal arts colleges relative to teacher preparation programs, and (5) examine the need for innovation and change in teacher preparation programs at liberal arts colleges. Recommendations for the future growth and development of these programs within liberal arts colleges are also made.

For the purpose of this discussion, the liberal arts college is defined as a college that is privately owned and operated, has independent status, is not dependent primarily on local, state, or federal funding, retains responsibility for establishing criteria for admission and retention of students, and has a curriculum that emphasizes the liberal arts as a foundation for all other professional and technical studies. Such institutions may be church related or supported or may be endowed by private funds. Liberal arts colleges that are part of public universities are not the subject of this discussion. This chapter examines small and mid-sized (fewer than 10,000 students) private or independent universities that train teachers.

Any discussion of liberal arts colleges must be undertaken with the understanding that as a group they represent great diversity in size, standards, quality of curriculum, mission, and governance. The one generalization that can be made regarding the colleges discussed is that they all train teachers.

Historical Overview

Liberal arts colleges have enjoyed a long tradition of excellence in education. Many trace their inauguration to religious idealists who, having found freedom in a new land, wanted to replicate the European classical liberal arts tradition. The new American liberal arts college became one where, in addition to celebrating the European model, new concepts related to "basic ideas of freedom, the dignity of the individual, and the rule of law rather than of men gained a foothold" (McGrath, 1975, p. 1).

Schmidt (1957) documented the evolution of the liberal arts college from its beginning in October 1636, when the charter for what was to become Harvard College was proposed by the General Court of Massachusetts Bay Colony, to the present model of the liberal arts college as an autonomous institution.

Initially, the new American colleges did not identify the preparation of teachers as an important mission. Haberman (1982) indicates that teacher training available in the young nation "was a form of apprenticeship of the 'sit-by-Nellie' variety" (p. 69). Few teachers in the colonial and postcolonial periods had little more than a secondary school education, if that. The first private normal school was founded in 1823, and the first teacher's seminary was established in Andover, Massachusetts, in the early 1830s. Men like Reverend Thomas Gallaudet and Reverend Samul R. Hall developed a curriculum that, while dependent on the liberal arts model (the European tridium), had distinctly evangelical priorities.

What did evolve from the private normal school experiment was the determination on the part of those shaping the future of liberal arts colleges that the preparation of teachers was a critical activity that could most effectively be carried on in the context of the liberal arts curriculum. The first state-supported normal school was established in Lexington, Massachusetts in 1839. Over time, the state-supported normal schools, which had sprung up around the nation, gradually disappeared as the baccalaureate degree became recognized as a minimal standard for entry into the profession and teacher education programs moved to teachers' colleges, liberal arts colleges, and public and private university settings.

The Impact of Governance

Because liberal arts colleges are generally smaller than their public counterparts, they tend to have a less bureaucratic governance structure, which makes possible greater involvement in curriculum and policy development. Faculty work more closely with each other and with central administrators than is possible in larger public institutions, where curriculum and policy development are frequently controlled by a state board of regents and there is limited opportunity to participate in governance at the institutional level.

In many larger public and private colleges and universities, preservice teacher training has come to be viewed as a low-prestige undertaking. This is especially true when schools of education must compete for resources with the more prestigious professional schools, such as medicine, law, engineering, and business. In these institutions, there is frequently a chasm of communication between the professional school and the arts and sciences; this does little to nurture the cooperative endeavors that are fundamental to the preparation of teachers.

The unique ethos of the liberal arts college results from governance structures that encourage cooperation rather than competition among colleagues. These structures result in an integration and organization of the curriculum that both respects the need for diversity and also promotes interdisciplinary cooperation, making the preparation of teachers a college-wide responsibility. It is this coherence of mission and goals that creates the optimal environment for teacher preparation.

The governance structure of liberal arts colleges, in addition to creating a climate of commonality and integration, is also characterized by an environment that emphasizes the importance of individual concerns and goals (both faculty and students); has a value-centered orientation; elicits loyalty (from both faculty and students), which results in greater support for institutional goals and objectives than occurs in large state institutions; and, by its very nature, has a more open atmosphere because its objectives are shared by most faculty and students.

These characteristics—integration, individualization, value-centered orientation, loyalty, and openness—have a liberating influence on teacher education programs at liberal arts colleges. Gideonse (1984) refers to liberal arts colleges as "intellectual communities," and indeed, when optimal factors are present, they replicate what is best in the democratic model of the community that "works."

There are those who believe that teacher education, when it becomes a college-wide or university-wide responsibility as it is in liberal arts colleges, is no one's responsibility. Their charge is that shared responsibility for teacher education may force the education faculty to be more dependent on others who are competing for the same resources. It is impossible to ensure that shared responsibility will not lead to lack of responsibility and diminution or dilution of resources. However, there is less chance that this will occur on smaller campuses, because in these settings teacher educators are involved in campus-wide governance. Of greater significance, perhaps, is the value placed on teacher education programs at liberal arts colleges. Although enrollments have dwindled, as is the case for all institutions that prepare teachers, in the liberal arts colleges teacher preparation is still valued intrinsically, and education faculty, for the most part, are viewed as equals in the community of scholars.

Curriculum Content

Recent studies issued by the Southern Regional Education Board (1985; Galambos, 1985) and the National Commission for Excellence in Teacher Education (1985) have reaffirmed the need for prospective teachers to complete a general education curriculum that is as strong as, or stronger than, that completed by students pursuing other majors. Liberal arts institutions are able to meet this need because they usually do not offer the broad array of electives and optional programs available at larger institutions and generally do not differentiate requirements. These characteristics produce a more clearly defined general education sequence and major and minor coursework than often results in large universities.

Unlike most state colleges and universities, liberal arts colleges require that prospective elementary teachers complete a substantive major in an academic area in addition to their elementary education program. This policy prepares them to teach the subjects that comprise the elementary school curriculum. Both the major and elementary planned programs are, in many liberal arts institutions, drawn from the coursework in the academic disciplines rather than being based in an education department.

In most liberal arts colleges instruction rather than research is the primary mission of the institution. Although research is valued in these colleges, the faculty's first responsibility is generally to teach students; teaching is not relegated to teaching assistants. Indeed, it is this characteristic that attracts students to liberal arts colleges and enriches their education.

Problems Confronting Liberal Arts Colleges

As recently as 1921, it was possible for individuals in thirty states to become certified to teach without meeting any minimum educational standards; fourteen states required only high school graduation and four states required some postsecondary training. Today, all states have established the baccalaureate degree as a minimum standard for certification.

States have established criteria for approval of teacher education programs, and thereby have had an impact on the content of those programs. The salutary effect of standards and program approval has been to provide teacher educators in both private and public institutions with leverage to marshal resources to implement state mandates and to sustain program integrity. The negative impact has been the inability of those responsible for teacher education programs to satisfy the demands of state, regional, and national criteria while at the same time attempting to deal with budgetary constraints and an already overcrowded curriculum.

Liberal arts colleges in particular have felt the impact of the demands of state, regional, and national accrediting standards. Students at liberal arts colleges are required to take the same general education courses as their peers in noneducation disciplines. Generally, they must then meet the same requirements for completion of majors and minors as all other students. This makes it particularly difficult to accommodate the imposition of the various standards for teacher education.

Sometimes teacher educators are forced to either expand the pedagogical component beyond the minimum requirements for the baccalaureate degree or to critically assess priorities in existing programs. This is particularly difficult for liberal arts colleges, where teacher education programs must usually be completed within the four-year degree program.

Funding and Resources. Liberal arts colleges, like all institutions, confront limitations on funding and resources that threaten their effectiveness. However, liberal arts colleges, because of their almost total dependence on tuition rather than on state or federal funds, have found it particularly difficult to deal with the recent declines in teacher education enrollments and other economic pressures.

Many liberal arts colleges have been forced to employ a greater number of adjunct faculty; this places additional burdens on full-time faculty, who already have heavy instructional, advisement, and program development or coordination responsibilities. Recent changes in teacher education standards enacted by states and regional and national accrediting agencies, while laudable, present problems for teacher educators in liberal arts colleges because these changes frequently require that faculty with special skills be employed and that courses be added to a curriculum already exceeding the requirements for the baccalaureate degree.

Updating the Curriculum. There are pressures to expand the clinical and student teaching experiences, to add material on educating the handicapped, to strengthen multicultural education, and a variety of other specialized areas. Although teacher educators in all institutions face the challenge of integrating new content into their programs while at the same time weeding out dated material, the incentive to do this is strongest in the liberal arts colleges. Liberal arts colleges usually do not have the option of expanding their programs beyond a fourth year. This constraint, rather than being a disadvantage, is a valuable pressure in liberal arts colleges to constantly update curriculum rather than to add to what may need to be revamped.

Innovation and Change in Teacher Preparation Programs

A shortage of teachers is imminent, and some regions of the country are already experiencing serious deficits. The demand for reform and higher standards comes at the same time as an equally compelling demand for more teachers, especially in critical shortage areas. Many liberal arts colleges are developing alternatives in teacher preparation to address these shortages. These have included internships and specialized programs for candidates with baccalaureate degrees who wish to become teachers. The alternative routes should not be viewed as a means of short circuiting the professional needs of prospective teachers. If that should happen, the call for reforms in teacher preparation will only intensify.

Looking to the Future

Recommendations based on future needs and present realities in teacher education in liberal arts colleges include the following:

Curriculum Development. Teacher educators in liberal arts colleges must become even more active in curriculum development. They should monitor curricular changes in general education and subject content, as well as in pedagogical content. They should become involved with local, state, and national agencies that mandate change in the way in which teachers are prepared.

Funding. Liberal arts teacher educators must be aggressive in identifying funding sources within and outside their institutions. This includes allocation of institutional funding, as well as federal, state, and foundational sources.

Professional Activities. Those responsible for teacher preparation programs in liberal arts colleges must become increasingly active in professional activities at all levels. The advantages of their programs are known to a limited number of people because their involvement in professional activities is generally also limited.

Research. While the "publish-or-perish" syndrome is less onerous in the liberal arts colleges than at larger public or private institutions, teacher educators at liberal arts colleges have a responsibility to contribute to the knowledge base of the profession. Liberal arts teacher educators must increase their contributions to research about teachers and teaching, particularly in liberal arts settings.

Cooperation. Liberal arts teacher educators must develop more effective information networks regarding successful programs and strategies related to recruitment, retention, and curriculum. Program evaluation and graduate follow-up models are examples of projects that could be shared.

Standards. Teacher educators must safeguard against the erosion of admission and retention standards and avoid compromises that may result in weakening the overall program requirements for prospective teachers. They should strengthen collaborative efforts with arts and sciences colleagues regarding the total curriculum for future teachers.

Conclusion

Liberal arts colleges have had a proud heritage of preparing teachers for the nation's schools. Teacher educators are drawn to these colleges because they represent an environment that facilitates the transmission of knowledge with a value-based orientation. This orientation enables faculty and students to move beyond the simple consideration of concepts and facts to an education that challenges. In this case, education becomes truly liberating.

Those who question the viability of liberal arts colleges to prepare teachers cannot ignore their long history of stability and contribution to the American way of life. Rainsford (1982) characterized them as institutions that "preserve that important element of diversity in American education that speaks to choice as well as skills" (p. 21). It is this element of diversity that mandates their continued contribution to staff our nation's schools—public and private—which also constitute a model of diversity.

References

Galambos, E. C. *Teacher Preparation: The Anatomy of a College Degree.* Atlanta, Ga.: Southern Regional Education Board, 1985.

Gideonse, H. D. "A Future Role for Liberal Arts Colleges in the Preparation of Teachers." In A. Tom (Ed.), *Teacher Education in Liberal Arts Settings: Achievements, Realities and Challenges.* Washington D.C.: American Association of Colleges for Teacher Education, 1984.

Haberman, M. "Research Needed on Direct Experience." In D. Corrigan, D. Palmer, and P. Alexander (Eds.), *The Future of Teacher Education: Needed Research and Practice.* College Station, Tex.: Texas A & M University, 1982.

McGrath, E. *Values, Liberal Education, and National Destiny.* Indianapolis, Ind.: Lily Endowment, 1975.

National Commission for Excellence in Teacher Education (NCETE). *A Call for Change in Teacher Education.* Washington D.C.: American Association of Colleges for Teacher Education, 1985.

Rainsford, G. "Small and Church-Related Is Beautiful." In J. C. Gies (Ed.), *Association of Governing Boards of Universities and Colleges Reports.* Washington D.C.: Association of Governing Boards of Universities and Colleges, January-February, 1982.

Schmidt, G. P. *The Liberal Arts College: A Chapter in American Cultural History.* New Brunswick, N.J.: Rutgers University Press, 1957.

Southern Regional Education Board (SREB). *Improving Teacher Education: An Agenda for Higher Education and the Schools.* Atlanta, Ga.: Southern Regional Education Board, 1985.

Norene F. Daly is dean of the College of Education, Florida Atlantic University. She has served as president of the Association of Independent Liberal Arts Colleges for Teacher Education and is president-elect of the American Association of Colleges for Teacher Education.

Shared views on ways to improve teacher education point the way to effective reform.

Common Directions Toward Improvement

Eva C. Galambos

What common ideas exist among the authors that lead to a consensus on how to improve the preparation of teachers? The following concerns surface repeatedly: (1) strengthening subject matter preparation, (2) providing better and more opportunities for education majors to try out teaching skills, (3) integrating theory and the results from the research on effective teaching into the professional education curriculum, and (4) cooperating with schools in preparing teachers.

Content in Teacher Education

Galambos, Scannell, Hawley, Gideonse, and Daly deal directly or indirectly with "content" in teacher education, and suggest various options for general education and subject-to-be-taught coverage. Galambos suggests that an insistence that freshman and sophomore general education courses represent college-level instead of high school–level work would in and of itself increase content preparation. The effect may be to extend teacher preparation for those students who must first succeed at noncredit remedial work before they may tackle the college curriculum. The extended program would still result in a baccalaureate degree, but one whose integrity has been restored.

Strengthening general education requires not only that college-level work be demanded of college students, but also that the configuration of subjects that represents general education be defined. In the American pluralistic higher education system, the "common core" will always be variously defined. However, it should be defined by the faculty of each college and university. In many institutions this will require narrowing the course choices in order to meet distribution requirements.

Greater prescriptiveness about the general education of teachers (or any students) will reduce electives and the extent to which students shape their education by pursuing their own interests. Smith (1980) suggests that "in a professional field where the academic preparation of students is closely associated with the work they are to do, as in the case of teachers, there is less room for the elective principle to function than in cases where the academic preparation is not closely associated with occupational responsibilities" (p. 37).

Although colleges of education have been under fire about the academic deficiencies of their graduates, the responsibility for defining a strengthened general education sequence rests primarily on the arts and sciences faculties. In theory, teacher education is guided on most campuses by a teacher education council, composed of education and arts and sciences faculty. Yet the participation by the arts and sciences representatives on these councils is weak in many institutions that prepare teachers.

As Galambos notes in Chapter One, two-thirds of teachers in training are transfer students. Community or two-year colleges play a major role in the education of teachers, as well as of other students. Strengthened content preparation, therefore, depends heavily on this sector of higher education. Yet a number of contradictory policies potentially intervene. Some states have moved toward an open door policy for two-year colleges, while at the same time raising standards for senior colleges. Where this is the case, the standards for the level of work expected of students, even in courses that have the same titles, may be vastly different. When statewide articulation agreements mandate that senior colleges must accept all transfer course credits from two-year colleges within the state, there are resultant problems in elevating general education standards.

Admission standards into teacher education programs that are keyed to the grade point averages that students have achieved in the lower division courses do not distinguish between the different levels of work a student may have completed in a two-year college that is related to the institution's own lower division courses. Obviously, reform of general education is a responsibility of arts and sciences as well as education faculty and of community colleges and their senior institutions.

Scannell foresees that more room can be gained for academic content by requiring extended or advanced preparation. However, in those five-year programs he describes, teaching field requirements have not expanded much, while pedagogy has. Hawley can find no evidence that substituting liberal arts electives for education courses will produce better teachers.

One of the questions concerning content is whether elementary teachers should complete an arts and sciences major, just as secondary teachers now do. Those supporting this requirement suggest that college students cannot develop a scholarly approach without pursuing some discipline in depth. Opponents point out that elementary school curriculum does not require depth in any subject in the early grades. Thus, two academic minors might be sufficient. Galambos questions why elementary teachers complete more social science college courses than they do in English and mathematics combined, when the latter two represent the heart of the basics in the early grades.

Secondary teachers already complete majors, but the issue of breadth versus depth for the configuration of their majors has not been resolved. Hawley suggests that the number of subject courses is not an issue. The usual major covers sufficient content, except for teaching advanced high school course sections. When a major is narrow, however, the usual ten to twelve courses may not be enough preparation for typical high school teaching assignments.

A physics major, for example, is likely to have taken enough chemistry courses so that he or she can teach both subjects. On the other hand, a biology major may not have taken enough chemistry or physics to be able to teach the other sciences. As the demographics of the 1980s take effect, high schools are becoming smaller. That means few high school teachers will have enough sections in one day to teach just one specialty. Many will also have to teach a related subject for some periods of each day. This trend suggests that secondary teachers take broader majors that cover related natural or social sciences. Can breadth *and* depth be accommodated in twelve courses? What are the trade-offs of these two options?

The task of defining majors that are appropriate for future secondary teachers cannot be undertaken alone either by state departments of education or by universities. Arts and sciences faculty in seeking to replicate their own education or to reflect their own specialized areas may be tempted to design majors too narrowly. (The author examined the minutes of a state council on teacher certification meeting and found the most frequent proponents for new, highly specialized certificate fields, such as drama or adaptive physical education, to be faculty in these fields.)

On the other hand, school personnel may be tempted to define certificate fields (and the corresponding majors) too broadly. A local superintendent, for example, has the least difficulty in meeting state regulations that mandate that teachers be assigned in the field if the teacher's field encompasses multiple subjects (social studies instead of history, geography, or political science, and science versus physics, chemistry, or biology.)

The resolution of tensions between depth and breadth of preparation for secondary teachers would be aided if state K-12 and higher education personnel had hard data available on what subjects high school teachers teach during their five- or six-period assignments. Few states, however, collect this information, and thus advisory groups on certification make decisions in a vacuum.

Gideonse points out that large universities tend to attract faculties with narrow interests; this impedes the development of a cohesive and well-defined curriculum in the arts and sciences. The analysis of general education by the Southern Regional Education Board in Chapter One relies entirely on large, state university programs. Would a transcript study of programs in smaller institutions have yielded evidence of a tighter general education curriculum? Daly certainly suggests this. Yet, these are the institutions that cannot meet the new quality standards, according to Gideonse. Perhaps the role of small liberal arts colleges in preparing teachers might fare better if extended or five-year programs were adopted. Then teachers could complete their liberal arts baccalaureates in these smaller institutions and transfer to other universities, if necessary, to complete a master's in education.

Accommodating the Practice of Teaching Skills

In follow-up studies, teacher education graduates have consistently rated student teaching as the most valuable part of their professional education programs. Several of the authors emphasize the importance of *applying* theory through actual *practice* of teaching skills. Nutter would achieve this objective within current teacher education programs by injecting more clinical applications. Dishner and Boothby would reinstate laboratory schools, although they do not go so far as to suggest that lab schools should be used for student teaching. The lab schools cannot match the student population diversity that teachers will encounter in the public schools. (Gideonse asserts that the teaching assignments for students in rural universities are incapable of providing a varied experience, since so many of the assignments are in rural schools. Yet, many of the teacher education programs with the largest resources are the very ones that are located outside of metropolitan areas! The urban universities are the latecomers in many states.)

Hawley explicitly questions how much meaning pedagogy courses have for future teachers before they have actually taught. He suggests making some methods courses part of in-school internships for beginning teachers. Other education courses might be postponed until graduate school—again after teachers have enough experience to appreciate the subject covered in such courses.

Foundations courses that cover the philosophy and history of education are courses that teachers generally rate low in their assessments of undergraduate teacher education. This no doubt reflects the lack of meaning such courses had before teachers became immersed in teaching. Just as business schools cover the theories of organizational behavior in graduate rather than undergraduate management courses (after students have some experience in the business world), so should education courses that deal with the larger institutional issues be offered at the inservice rather than preservice level.

One of the charges that has been leveled against colleges of education is that their graduate offerings differ very little from their undergraduate ones. Hawley suggests that these graduate courses are not known as "more rigorous than the undergraduate ones" (p. 47). Approximately half of all teachers in the United States hold master's degrees, and most of these are in education.

Kerr (1983) suggests two reasons why graduate programs are merely extensions of the undergraduate programs, rather than sophisticated professional offerings: (1) the National Council for Accreditation of Teacher Education standards at the postgraduate level do not effectively link practice to research, and (2) the faculty of graduate programs are primarily those who were shifted out of the under-enrolled baccalaureate programs.

A deliberate shift of foundations courses from the undergraduate to the graduate level would provide an opportunity for serious revisions of these courses. There then would be time for students to read and discuss original writings by important contributors to the philosophy of education, rather than to have to read excerpts or synopses in crowded undergraduate courses. Graduate students could be expected to explore educational issues in some depth instead of dutifully following syllabi and outlines that leave them with little understanding.

Schlechty and Whitford take the full leap. They maintain that injecting more clinical application into existing programs is not the answer. The only way to learn how to teach is to practice it *in the schools.* They specify that such schools, or "academies," would not resemble current institutions. A new type of organization should be created. Hawley suggests that the creation of such academies is gaining acceptance. Might this be the option that will unite those who now disagree about the need to extend teacher education to fifth-year programs?

Integrating Research and Theory

Galambos questions the current number of methods courses (those that deal with the techniques and materials of teaching various elementary school subjects). Would it not be possible to consolidate separate courses on methods of teaching language arts, arithmetic, social studies, science, art, reading, and even physical education? Are there not some generic methods that could apply to each field?

This then leads to the question of whether a knowledge base exists in teacher education. If certain principles have been established that describe the teaching/learning process, then given a particular set of circumstances, these principles should lead to generic methods or techniques. A profession is generally recognized as such only after it is grounded in theories that are predictive of outcomes. If such theories have been developed, pedagogy courses should cover them, as well as the evidence that led to them. Such courses would be quite other than courses of the accumulated lore or discrete techniques of teaching of each and every subject at various grade levels that now prevail.

Smith, in his landmark work, *A Design for a School of Pedagogy* (1980), addresses the issue of a knowledge base in education. He distinguishes between scientific findings that explain the cause-and-effect relationships of learning from means-ends relationships that correlate teacher behavior variables and student learning. Although pedagogy may not yet contain knowledge on causes and effects, Smith argues that it has accumulated a store of important findings at the means-ends range of knowledge.

The problem, as Smith sees it (1980), is that "pedagogical faculties largely ignore research findings as they train school personnel, especially teachers and administrators" (p. 54) and that "some are familiar with research in teaching but make no use of it. Others try to apply it but do not know how, or else find they have no resources for doing so. By far the largest number know nothing about it, and some claim it does not exist" (p. 83).

Numerous teacher educators attest that during the last decade, important research has been completed that should find its way into the undergraduate pedagogy curriculum (Egbert and Kluender, 1984; Berliner, 1985). Popular buzz words such as "with-it-ness," "time-on-task," and "school climate" result from this recent body of educational research. The ultimate value of the findings of these studies will be tested over time as they are applied to real situations. A cynic might ask, "What is so new about the detailed findings that show that children learn more if they spend more time engaged in academic tasks?" However, if detailed documentation of this sort does improve the utilization of classroom time and pupils' achievement levels, the incorporation of such research in teacher education will have proven its worth.

Berliner is a strong advocate for the new research, which he characterizes as "sensible and replicable findings and a newer and richer set of concepts to analyze classroom phenomena" (1985, p. 19). He suggests that this material could be included in the so-called curriculum laboratories or methods courses. "Nationally, most such curriculum laboratories, where one can learn the content in an area, the time allocations that might be necessary to teach particular parts of the curriculum, and the tests for specific curriculum materials are really just 'rooms' where one can go through materials and catalogues of different publishers" (1985, p. 19).

He would transform these methods courses into analytical ones, presumably incorporating research findings.

Scannell suggests that extended programs will provide more time for covering the new research on effective teaching. Will this new material be added to the current configuration of methods courses or will it replace them? A serious issue that deserves more atttention is how colleges of education can overcome rigidities that prevent substitution of new courses for discredited or outmoded courses. In the climate of declining enrollments, with a 50 percent reduction of undergraduates in teacher education in the last decade, faculty members are often afraid to risk serious curriculum reform that might endanger their own offerings. Given the normal inertia that exists in most academic departments, it is unlikely that serious curriculum reform will occur in the colleges of education unless financial incentives or "hold-harmless" guarantees to protect faculty are provided.

Is there a contradiction between the repeated advocacy of more clinical experience in teacher education versus the call to inject research findings, or, as Hawley suggests, to prepare teachers "to use theory as a tool for learning and inventing"? Can teacher education become both more practical and yet be based to a greater extent on research and theory? How are both directions to be accommodated? Must this be done simultaneously? This is a perennial issue. The tension between theory and practice has certainly troubled many professions and will continue to create debate in educational circles.

Cooperating Institutions

While there is disagreement among authors about the length of formal education needed to accommodate both theory and practice, a nebulous consensus may be developing. Schlechty would shift the practical applications of learning how to teach to school settings. Hawley stresses the need for much greater support of beginning teachers during their induction period and suggests that methods courses be shifted to that stage. One extended (or master's level) teacher education program established by Memphis State University in 1984 is an example of this approach. This program includes a nine-month internship during which student teachers learn methods in the schools and gradually assume increasing responsibility. Perhaps the issue is narrowing to one of whether beginning teachers, as they learn skills on the job, should be classified as students who generate college credits or whether they are trainees of the schools and should be paid trainee salaries. In either case, greater utilization of schools to prepare teachers, whether as students, inductees, or trainees, depends on more cooperation between higher education and the schools. Such cooperation is essential, regardless of whether a new institution is created outside the direct control of either group or the current institutional arrangements are maintained.

Schlechty alone recognizes the role of master teachers in preparing new teachers. For years, cooperating or supervising teachers have spent considerably more time observing and assisting student teachers during internships than have the education professors, to whose credit student teaching hours accrue. Schlechty's proposal would finally formalize and reward the contribution of those who are truly "master" teachers. There is no reason, however, why these teachers could not be rewarded even under the current institutional arrangements or within the newly developing career ladder plans for teachers.

The Need for Outcome Data

A shortcoming of this volume is the lack of outcome data that would justify any of the positions taken by the authors. Do teachers who know more about a subject do a better job with students than those who know less? What type of program (extended or four-year, one that meets national accreditation standards or one that does not, one that stresses theory or one that stresses classroom teaching skills) is associated with the highest outcomes in terms of student learning? Hawley's prescription for evaluation of change before wholesale moves are made in any one direction makes sense. Although deregulation is threatening, especially if regulation has served as a protection against competition, judicious deregulation and experimentation in teacher education—*with* rigorous evaluation—constitutes a powerful alternative to the status quo.

A pluralistic approach to reforming teacher education has some advantages over wholesale adoption of any one model. Most observers agree that a teacher shortage is imminent. The shortage becomes obvious when the numbers of newly graduating teachers are compared with those who are leaving the profession; this may be mitigated by the fact that some previously trained teachers who left the profession may reenter it. In view of some level of impending teacher shortage, the near future will be a difficult time to severely restrict the entry route to teaching, either by requiring advanced degrees or by reducing the number of institutions where teachers are produced. The teaching profession has been able, despite the low pay, to attract entrants because educational opportunities for entry into the field have been so widely available. Proximity of educational facilities tends to reduce the costs to students.

In the absence of outcome data about the various directions in which teacher education can move, no wholesale changes are indicated. Instead, pilot programs should be established, with careful evaluation of these and of control programs. The advantage of the pluralistic higher and public education system in this nation is that it presents opportunities to test new directions. This pluralism ensures that more than one model to improve teacher education will be tried. However, it does not ensure the concurrent design of an evaluation plan to produce comparative outcome data. As the federal government retreats from direct to indirect involvement in education, one role it might well pursue is as a catalyst for coordinating a serious evaluation of models to improve teacher education.

References

Berliner, D. "Laboratory Settings and the Study of Teacher Education." Paper presented at the American Educational Research Association, Chicago, Illinois, March 1985.

Egbert, R. L., and Kluender, M. M. *Using Research To Improve Teacher Education: The Nebraska Consortium.* (Teacher Education Monograph no. 1). Washington, D.C.: ERIC Clearinghouse on Teacher Education, 1984.

Kerr, D. H. "Teaching Competence and Teacher Education in the United States." *Teachers College Record,* Spring 1983, p. 525.

Smith, B. O. *A Design for a School of Pedagogy.* Washington, D.C.: Department of Education, 1980.

Eva C. Galambos is consultant to the Southern Regional Education Board. She served as staff director of that organization's Task Force on Higher Education and the Schools from 1981 to 1985.

Index

A

Academy for Excellence in Teaching and Educational Leadership: concerns about, 44-45; feasibility of, 45-46; mission of, 42-44
Ahern, J. F., 68
American Association of Colleges for Teacher Education (AACTE), 21, 25, 27, 28, 36, 70, 71, 72, 81
Anderson, R. D., 33, 36
Association of American Colleges (AAC), 19, 25
Association of Colleges and Schools of Education in State Universities and Land Grant Colleges and Affiliated Private Universities, 7
Austin College, extended program at, 20
Ayers, Q. R., 7, 15

B

Bates, G. W., 63, 67
Bell, T., 70n
Berliner, D. C., 20, 25, 96, 99
Biles, B. L., 40, 46
Billups, L. H., 46
Boothby, P. R., 2, 49, 57, 94
Borg, W. R., 63, 67
Brinler, P. S., 57, 68
Browne, K. A., 50, 57
Bush, W .S., 63, 67
Butler, N. M., 50

C

California, postbaccalaureate training required in, 27, 32
Chicago, University of: Laboratory School at, 50; postbaccalaureate teacher training at, 27
Chion-Kenney, L., 55, 56
Clark, D. L., 41, 46
Cliff, R., 35, 36
Clinical approach: Advocated, 59-68; background on, 59-60; concept of, 59; examples of, 62-64; integration of, 61-62; principles of, 60-62; requirements for, 65-67; in rural areas, 78-79; sequencing in, 60-61; supervision in, 61
Cobb, P., 63, 67
Coleman, J., 7, 15
Commission on Teacher Education, 29
Cornett, L. M., 15, 36
Corrigan, D. C., 26, 46
Cremin, L. A., 23, 25
Cruickshank, D. R., 51, 57
Currence, C., 70, 81-82
Curriculum, of liberal arts colleges, 86, 87, 88

D

Daly, N. F., 2, 3, 83, 90, 91, 94
Dartmouth College, and extended program, 30
Denmark, G. W., 26, 46
Dewey, J., 50, 56, 57
Dishner, E. K., 2, 49, 57, 94
Dreeben, R., 38, 46
Drucker, P. F., 46
Druva, C. A., 33, 36

E

Education Commission of the States, 80
Egbert, R. L., 96, 99
Emory University, and extended programs, 30
Evertson, C., 34, 36
Extended programs: advocated, 17-26; background on, 17-18, 27-28; conclusions on, 25, 35-36; critical view of, 27-36; and criticism of teacher education, 18-19; economic costs of, 30-31; features of, 19-21; individual costs of, 28-29; as predominant model, 22-24; and quality

Extended programs: *(continued)* of teaching, 31-34; rationale for, 21-22; risks of mandating, 28-31; and teacher shortage, 13, 24-25

F

Faculty: inquiry by, 77, 88; as models of practice, 77-78; numbers of, 74-76; professional activities of, 88
Feistritzer, E. C., 7, 15, 65, 68, 71
Flexner, A., 45, 56
Florida, University of, extended program at, 20, 27
Flowers, J. G., 59, 68
Friedman, M. I., 51, 57, 62, 68

G

Gage, N. L., 20, 25
Galambos, E. C., 3, 5, 15, 19, 25, 34, 36, 86, 91, 92, 95, 99
Gall, M., 67
Gallaudet, T., 84
Gallegos, A., 19, 25
General education: amount and kind of, 8-9; analysis of status of, 5-15; in baccalaureate programs, 13-15; background on, 5; conclusion on, 15; defining, 7-8; and distribution requirements, 11-13; level of courses in, 9-11; need for, 6-7. *See also* Liberal arts colleges
General Motors, Saturn plant of, 41
Gibney, T. C., 68
Gideonse, H. D., 2-3, 21, 25, 69, 76, 78, 80, 82, 85, 89, 91, 94
Goodlad, J. I., 52, 54, 57
Governance, of liberal arts colleges, 85-86
Governor's Center for Educational Innovation and Technology, 55
Green, T., 72, 82
Griffin, G. A., 61, 68

H

Haberman, M., 84, 89
Hall, G. E., 65, 68
Hall, S. R., 84
Harvard University, and teacher training, 30, 84

Hawaii, University of, laboratory school of, 53
Hawley, W. D., 1-2, 27, 36, 91, 93, 94, 95, 97, 98
Hayes, P. B. D., 57, 68
Holmes Group, 27, 34, 70
Hovda, R. A., 40, 46
Howd, M. C., 50, 57
Howsam, R. B., 26, 39, 46
Hunter, M., 49, 52, 56, 57
Hutchinson, C. M. P., 63, 67
Hutton, H., 50, 57

I

IBM, training program by, 38
Inglis, J. D., 64, 68
Institutional reduction: advocated, 69-82; background on, 69-70; and faculty, 74-78; and liberal education, 76; reasons for, 70-71; and rural clinical sites, 78-79; and standards, 74-79
Ishler, P., 62, 68
Ishler, R. E., 7, 15

J

Johns Hopkins University, Medical School of, 45
Johnston, J. M., 61, 68
Jones, H. L., 65, 68
Journal of Teacher Education, 27, 36
Joyce, B., 35, 36

K

Kansas, University of, extended program at, 20, 27
Kelley, M. L., 67
Kelly, E. H., 50, 57
Kerchner, C. T., 32, 36
Kerr, D. H., 95, 99
Kindsvatter, R., 65, 68
Kluender, M. M., 96, 99
Kyle, D. W., 40, 46

L

Laboratory schools: advocated, 49-57; background on, 49-50; conclusions on, 54-56; decline of, 50-51;

development of, 50-51; example of, 53-54; research preparation role of, 51-52
Langer, P., 67
Leinhardt, G., 34, 36
Liberal arts colleges, private: analysis of teacher education in, 83-90; background on, 83-84; conclusion on, 89; curriculum of, 86, 87, 88; defined, 83; and extended programs, 30; funding of, 87, 88; future of, 88-89; governance of, 85-86; history of, 84; innovation in, 88; and institutional reduction, 76; problems of, 86-88; and standards, 89. *See also* General education
Lindsey, M., 68
Lortie, D. C., 40, 46, 60, 68
Louisiana Board of Regents, 6, 15

M

McGee, G. W., 50, 52, 53, 57
McGrath, E., 84, 89
McPherson, R. B., 50, 52, 53, 57
Malcolm Price Laboratory School, 53-54
Manski, C., 30, 36
Marker, B., 41, 46
Massachusetts, liberal colleges in, 84
Mastain, R., 70, 82
Memphis State University, extended program of, 97
Mergendoller, J. R., 40, 47
Microcomputer Curriculum Project, 54
Mills, J. R., 62, 68

N

Nash, R. J., 26, 46
National Academy for Teacher Education, 55
National Association of State Directors of Teacher Education and Certification, 71
National Association of State Universities and Land-Grant Colleges (NASULGC), 19, 26
National Center for Education Statistics (NCES), 30, 70-71, 79
National Center for Educational Information, 71
National Commission for Excellence in Teacher Education (NCETE), 5, 7, 15, 27, 54, 55, 57, 86, 89
National Council for the Accreditation of Teacher Education (NCATE), 70, 71, 72, 73*n*, 75, 78, 80, 82, 95
National Education Association (NEA), 7, 72, 82
National Institute of Education (NIE), 19, 26
National Teacher Examination, 6-7
New Hampshire, University of, extended program at, 20
Nielsen, R., 53, 54, 57
Nixon, J. A., 40, 46
North Carolina, SAT and NTE scores in, 6-7
Northern Iowa, University of, laboratory school of, 53-54
Nutter, N., 2, 59, 68

O

Oberlin College, and extended program, 30
Ohio, teacher education faculty in, 74-75
Orlosky, D. E., 64, 68
Orr, P., 73, 74, 82

P

Patterson, A. D., 68
Peseau, B., 73, 74, 82
Plisko, V. W., 30, 31, 36
Project IMPACT, 54
Public Law 94-142, 19
Public schools: and Academy for Excellence, 42, 44, 45; reform proposed for, 37-47

R

Rainsford, G., 89
Reed College, and extended programs, 30
Reform: action sharing for, 37-47; background on, 37-40; need for, 40-41; proposal for, 41-46

Reynolds, M. C., 26
Rice University, and extended program, 30
Roth, R. A., 70, 82
Ryan, K., 61, 68

S

Scannell, D. P., 1, 17, 26, 91, 92, 97
Schaff, J., 68
Schlechty, P. C., 2, 35, 37, 45, 46, 47, 95, 98
Schmidt, G. P., 84, 89
Scholastic Aptitude Test (SAT), 6-7
Sharp, B. L., 19, 26
Simon, H. A., 82
Sizer, T. R., 49, 52, 57
Smith, B. O., 20, 23, 26, 80, 82, 92, 96, 99
Smith, D., 34, 36
Smith, D. C., 20, 26
Southern Regional Education Board (SREB), 7, 10, 86, 89, 94
Southern states, general education survey in, 5-15
Spitler, H. D., 15, 36
Standards: and institutional reduction, 74-79; and liberal arts colleges, 89; for teacher education, 72-74
Stanford University, postbaccalaureate teacher education at, 27
Stratemeyer, F. B., 68
Swarthmore College, and extended programs, 30

T

Teacher Corps, 51
Teacher education: and Academy for Excellence, 43, 44, 46; clinical approach to, 59-68; concerns about, 1; content in, 91-94; criticisms of, 18-19; extended programs for, 17-36; and general education, 5-15; improvement of, 91-99; institutional reduction for, 49-57; in liberal arts colleges, 83-90; practice of skills in, 94-95; reform proposed for, 37-47; research and theory integrated in, 95-97; research needed on, 98-99; standards for, 72-74; status of, 39-40
Teacher's associations, and Academy for Excellence, 43-44, 45
Teachers College: mission of, 50; postbaccalaureate training at, 27
Tikunoff, W. J., 40, 47
Tom, A. R., 72, 82
Treiman, D. J., 32, 36
Tucker, S. B., 69n, 70n, 82
Tulane, University, and extended program, 30
Tyler, R., 29, 36

U

United Automobile Workers, 41
U.S. Bureau of the Census, 71, 82

V

Varina High School, 55
Veitch, S. C., 46
Virginia, laboratory school in, 55

W

Waller, W., 39, 47
Washington University, and extended program, 30
Weaver, T. T., 7, 15
Whitford, B. L., 2, 37, 40, 47, 95
Wilen, W., 65, 68

Z

Zlotnik, M., 36
Zuckerman, R. A., 63, 68